TRANSMITTING INFORMATION THROUGH MANAGEMENT AND UNION CHANNELS

Two Case Studies

By

Helen Baker, *Associate Director*

John W. Ballantine

and

John M. True

formerly Research Assistants
Industrial Relations Section

1949

INDUSTRIAL RELATIONS SECTION

DEPARTMENT OF ECONOMICS AND SOCIAL INSTITUTIONS

PRINCETON UNIVERSITY, PRINCETON, NEW JERSEY

INDUSTRIAL RELATIONS SECTION
DEPARTMENT OF ECONOMICS AND SOCIAL INSTITUTIONS
PRINCETON UNIVERSITY
Established 1922

J. Douglas Brown, Director
Helen Baker, Associate Director
Hazel C. Benjamin, Librarian

———

Richard A. Lester, Research Associate
Robert L. Aronson, Research Assistant
Robert R. France, Research Assistant
Fred Slavick, Research Assistant

The reports of the Industrial Relations Section are the joint product of the Section's staff under the supervision of the Director. In the case of each report, the research and preparation of manuscript is done by the staff members whose names appear on the title page.

Research Report Series: No. 79

FOREWORD

COMMUNICATIONS in an industrial corporation, as in an army, is *organization in action*. The plan of organization in most corporations is designed to reflect lines of responsibility and authority. Since structure is easier to visualize than action, a carefully developed organization chart has become a symbol of sound administration. But often a neat and consistent pattern of descending lines of authority covers up grave difficulties in securing rapid understanding, acceptance, and action when more than routine orders are involved. It is the function of effective communications to resolve these difficulties so that the corporation, to survive, can react quickly to changing conditions wherever and whenever they may arise.

A subtle hazard in the analysis of communications within a human organization is the too easy analogy to communications in terms of physical transmission. The closing of a single switch may light a city. A newspaper headline appears on thousands of stands and doorsteps within a few hours. But to transmit to the inhabitants of a city the meaning of a new idea may take a decade. Fortunately cities can survive much ignorance, inertia, and misunderstanding. They are among the hardiest of human organizations. An industrial corporation, however, is concerned with the far more difficult task of extending the physical transmission of information into intelligent action and attitude. The written or spoken word, like the telephone, remains but the *tool* of communication in its effort to secure understanding and response.

An age-old problem in communication is the different meanings which common words may have to different people. It required the parable of the Good Samaritan twenty centuries ago to assure an understanding of the simple word "neighbor." Such attractive words as "cooperative," "fair," "friendly," and "responsible" are loose aggregations of concepts which each person interprets in the light of his own experience. It is in the highly important area of evaluative words that meanings most often go to sea. Yet it is in just this area that accurate communication is most necessary if human organization is to be effective.

The best solution of this core problem in communication seems to lie in the participation of the transmitter and the receiver of information or ideas in a give-and-take discussion. In such discussion, meanings are questioned, corrected, and refined, misunderstandings are uncovered, and attention is focussed upon the *idea* which lies behind the word, rather than upon the word itself. But such discussion is not easy to assure. It requires intelligent direction, incisive questioning, and ready use of telling illustration. It is the essence of good teaching and effective communication.

The following report has absorbed much time and effort in its preparation. It has involved hours and days of work for the officers of the two corporations and the two unions who cooperated most generously in its development. The Section has been increasingly convinced of the deep significance of the problem of effective communications if American industry is to be blessed with constructive labor relations. It realizes that the report is but a small beginning and that the conclusions it reaches are, at most, tentative.

J. Douglas Brown
Director

Princeton, New Jersey
August 19, 1949

CONTENTS

CASE STUDY TWO: ESSO STANDARD OIL COMPANY
(BAYWAY REFINERY) AND THE INDEPENDENT
PETROLEUM WORKERS

CONTENTS

Tables in Case Study One

Tables in Case Study Two

I. INTRODUCTION

A. Background of the Problem

A SYSTEM for transmitting and receiving information up and down through all levels is a basic requirement for any organization that depends upon human cooperation. The problem of communications is particularly acute in the industrial organization where the need is for effective coordinated action by many dissimilar groups. The industrial executive, the union leader, or the employee on the production line needs no more evidence of the urgency of this problem than his daily experience in receiving inadequate information or failing to make someone else understand his point of view. Attitude surveys among foremen and employees have shown lack of knowledge and understanding of the objectives and policies of companies of which they are a part. Similar misunderstanding exists on the part of top executives failing to recognize the needs and objectives of their employees. Unauthorized strikes, frequently without apparent justification, have given dramatic emphasis to the need for a more timely and more adequate exchange of information. The apparent ineffectiveness of communications in industry has lately become one of the most discussed problems of industrial relations.

Why this recent upsurge of interest in industrial communications? Many students of industrial relations have stressed the influence of size on the problem. The big corporation, it is said, has so many levels in the organizational hierarchy from the decision-maker to the worker that only with utmost care can understanding be gained throughout the organization. Yet blocks to the effective exchange of information may be more frequent and as serious in the small organization. Moreover, bigness and complexity are not new factors. Companies, in fact, have long been of a size to make communications a complex process. Current interest in the process of industrial communications cannot be attributed to the newness of the problem, but may be explained in terms of a combination of circumstances that have recently brought the problem of communications to the forefront of the industrial relations scene.

The rapid increase in unionization in the thirties undoubtedly was an important factor. A newly established union in a plant in itself generates a greater demand for information. It also allows employees to express, perhaps for the first time, dissatisfaction with the amount or kind of information given them. Union statements often are not in accord with management's view of a situation. Management's statements are subject to challenge. To give its employees what it feels to be the facts of a specific case and to maintain in general the favorable opinion of its workers, industry has found it necessary to pay much more attention than previously to what is told employees and how it is told.

Governmental rulings, which for a few years exerted some restraint upon management's communication with its employees, also made management more conscious of its rights and responsibilities in this area. Wartime conditions, such as limitations upon management's right to discharge and the tighter labor market, made the industrial executive consider means of gaining employee interest and cooperation rather than depend upon discipline. Trends in personnel administration, in general, and such developments as the Hawthorne experiments, in particular, influenced executives to think of organizational effectiveness in terms of human relations and mutual understanding. The present world political situation, along with the collectivist challenge to the enterprise system, has convinced many industrial leaders that industry must demonstrate to its own members the benefits of capitalism if that system is to survive.

Thus a combination of these factors and others has highlighted the problem of communications that has always existed. With the greater awareness of the problem, attempts at a solution have also multiplied.

B. Approaches to the Problem

Communications in an industrial organization are as varied and complex as the organization itself. The approach to improved communications has rarely been to view the problem as a whole but rather from the angle of one or another special interest. The outside researcher has analyzed the problem and recommended action according to his particular background. The sociologist interested in the application of social concepts to industry, the psychologist attempting to apply scientific measurements to human relationships, the educator studying the process of learning, the specialist concerned with organizational theory, and the publicist seeking improved techniques for influencing people, all have given considerable attention to this subject of communications and all have contributed in varying degree to an understanding of its total complex nature.

Within industry, individuals and groups have suggested ways and means of improvement or have handled communications according to their particular needs. The line executives have viewed it as an operational problem, the employee relations staff as a matter of human relationships or collective bargaining, the training director as proof of the need for more training, and the public relations man as a matter of getting an impressive story to the people at the right time. In companies in which these various special interests have been assigned to the problem one by one, improvements have been spotty and spasmodic. The companies that have tried to coordinate the various activities related to communications have gained the greatest insight into the nature of the problem and developed the most constructive programs to meet it.

The Industrial Relations Section, in the recent past, has studied communications as a problem in gaining understanding of industrial relations policies.[1] The study was approached from the point of view of management's desire for understanding and an analysis of the procedures followed in an attempt to gain company-wide understanding. While interviewing executives in connection with that study, it became evident that the concept that management, without consideration of the union, could work out satisfactory methods of gaining employee understanding was unrealistic for situations in which a union was involved. A considerable majority of executives reporting for 84 companies felt that the union had had a marked influence, either positive or negative, on managements' efforts to communicate with their employees.[2]

As indications of the complexity of communications developed, the Section considered the value of studying the functions of management and union in the total process of communications in one or more specific industrial situations. The result was the study of communications first in the New Brunswick plants of Johnson & Johnson and later in the Bayway refinery of the Esso Standard Oil Company.

C. Objectives of the Case Studies

The two case studies sought to provide, through close observation of the process of communication in a given industrial situation, insight into the structure of the communication system as well as the substance of communications, and to seek some measure of their effectiveness in terms of individual and group attitudes. In both cases the employees were represented by a union. The studies were undertaken with a view of communications not as a straight line from top echelon to employee, nor as two parallel, up-and-down lines, but as a circuit connecting the various levels of management and the union and both of these with one another and the employees.

Because communications are so closely interwoven with other activities of an industrial organization, it was necessary to determine in advance what the study should exclude as well as what it should cover. It

[1] Industrial Relations Section, Research Report No. 78. Company-wide Understanding of Industrial Relations Policies. 1948.
[2] *Ibid.* Chapter V, especially p. 43.

was clear that communication was an integral part of union-management relations, of the application of personnel policies and the labor contract, of employee attitudes, and of production operations. All of these phases of industry, it was recognized, would have to be touched upon, but none of them was to be studied except as a background for understanding their influences on communication and, in turn, the influence of communication on them.

Specific aims were to observe and analyze:

(1) the objectives of management and union in their informational efforts
(2) media and channels being used (including line and staff personnel)
(3) the attitude of the personnel in the middle and lower levels of the organizations towards upper level objectives and their own responsibilities in maintaining communications
(4) the type of information employees want from the management and the union
(5) the varying effectiveness of the media in terms of employee interest in and knowledge of specific subjects.

These general and specific aims were followed for both studies, with some variation in method as a result of the experience with the first study and because of differences in the two situations, especially the differences in size of company and type of union.[1] It is hoped that the findings reported in the following chapters will be helpful to many organizations in analyzing their own problems of communications and in developing effective solutions. However, in considering the applicability of these findings to other situations, those responsible for planning should not fail to take into account the objectives of these studies and the characteristics of the two environments within which observations were made.

[1] For a discussion of methods, see Appendix B, page 137.

CASE STUDY ONE:

JOHNSON & JOHNSON AND LOCAL 630, TEXTILE WORKERS UNION OF AMERICA

II. BACKGROUND OF THE CASE

A. THE COMPANY

J[OHNSON & JOHNSON, the world's largest producer of surgical dressings, also manufactures a variety of other products including filter products, industrial tape, diapers, baby powders, elastic goods, and toothbrushes.]Operating more than 18 domestic manufacturing plants and employing more than 10,000 persons, the company is actually an aggregation of small industries and relatively small plants. More than 12 of its manufacturing establishments are located in New England, New Jersey, Georgia, and Chicago. Several mills are operated in foreign countries to feed the company's world-wide system of distribution. Aggregate sales for all operations in 1946 exceeded the $100,000,-000 level for the first time in the company's history.

[Established by Robert W. Johnson in 1873, the company began its operations in New Brunswick, New Jersey, in 1885. From that time until 1943, both ownership and management of the corporation remained in the control of the Johnson family. In 1943, securities were placed on public sale on the New York Stock Exchange but the management of the corporation remains under the active control of the Johnson family.]General Robert W. Johnson, son of the founder, is the present chairman of the board of directors. The nerve-center of Johnson & Johnson's manufacturing and management operations remains in the company's first and oldest plant, located in New Brunswick, New Jersey, where the company occupies an outstanding position in the industrial life of the community.

The major portion of this study deals with communications in the company's largest plant which adjoins the executive offices in New Brunswick. The plant is organized into three manufacturing divisions, the cotton mill, the gauze mill, and the plaster mill. The average employment for the plant for 1947, including production and office workers, was around 2600. Total employment as of May, 1947, in operating jobs in the three production mills on the home lot was 937 persons. Each of the mills is headed by a superintendent who reports to the vice president of manufacturing. The vice president is responsible to the president of the company. The management organization in New Brunswick is characterized by the ease with which operating management can contact top management.

Two aspects of the departmental organization within the New Brunswick plant are worth noting. Each mill is organized into sub-departments, each of which is headed by a foreman. Foremen have their own offices and technical staffs of production coordinators, clerks, and industrial engineers, and, in general, have considerable authority and prestige. A second, and rather unique, feature of the supervisory organization is the decentralization of the industrial engineering staff. This staff is especially important because a large proportion of the wage earners at the Johnson & Johnson mills are paid on a piece-work or incentive basis. Although the industrial engineering function had formerly been centralized, as is the present personnel department, it was decentralized in 1944 in order to make it a more direct tool of supervisory management.

Communications were also studied in the Ethicon Suture Laboratories plant, located some three miles outside of New Brunswick. This plant, employing 111 operating personnel in May, 1947, is the embodiment of two basic policies strongly advocated by the chairman of the board: namely, physical and managerial decentralization, and the beautification of industrial establishments. The chief difference between management's communications system for Ethicon Suture and the New Brunswick plant is the much more extensive use of a plant broadcasting system in the former.

Personnel activities in both the New Brunswick and Ethicon Suture plants are closely coordinated by the company's central personnel department. Although functioning in a staff relationship with operating management and without direct authority, this department has extensive influence in the two plants. Its prestige may be attributed both to the support the department receives from the company's top management and to the sincerity and ability of the director of personnel. The director of personnel is a member of the board of directors and reports directly to the president of the company.

B.   THE UNION

Although Johnson & Johnson employees in New Brunswick had organized an independent union in 1942, they had little experience with collective bargaining until 1944 when Local 630 of the Textile Workers Union of America (CIO) won bargaining rights. In 1947, Johnson & Johnson workers in three of the five plants in the New Brunswick area (and in all of the units covered by this study) were represented by Local 630. One of the other plants was organized by the Paper Makers (AFL), and an adjoining plant was non-union.

The organization and growth of Local 630 was neither spectacular nor particularly easy. When the Local was recognized in 1944 it had won by a plurality of only 189 over the independent union in a total of 1853 votes. From the start, Johnson & Johnson management at the top level sought to build a cooperative relationship with the union. Aside from several more or less spontaneous and brief work stoppages in 1945 over the issue of the union shop, no strikes or major disturbances have occurred. Maintenance of membership and the check-off were obtained when the union was first recognized. After several months of negotiations, the union shop was secured in 1946 and, at the same time, the company and union agreed to their first two-year contract. Despite the absence of strife in union-management relations, the officers have not had an easy time in welding their membership into a strong union.

The functional organization of Local 630 is typical of other locals in the Textile Workers Union. Union officers and shop stewards are elected annually, the officers at a mass membership meeting and the stewards by the workers in each department. Meetings for the entire membership are normally held once a month and more frequently when necessary. The executive board, composed of all the elected officers and shop stewards, and the highest governing body within the local, meets monthly, the officers meet weekly.

Along with seven other T.W.U.A. unions in the New Brunswick area, Local 630 is affiliated with the Central Jersey Joint Board. The Joint Board employs a business agent, coordinates the activities of its affiliated locals, provides centralized office and accounting service, promotes labor education through its educational director, and acts as the direct representative of the national union at the local level. Delegates from each local are elected to serve on the executive board of the Joint Board. This body, in turn, elects officers and holds meetings at least monthly. The Joint Board's business manager, also a member of the Central Executive Board, is appointed by the general president of the national union, subject to the approval of the Joint Board delegates. In actual fact, the business manager is the key figure not only in the administration of the day-to-day affairs of the affiliated local unions, but also in the formulation of local union policies and in collective bargaining negotiations.

III. THE COMPANY'S
INFORMATIONAL PROGRAM

A. PRINCIPAL OBJECTIVES

THE Johnson & Johnson informational program for employees
is but one part of a carefully planned program to build an indus-
try-community situation that will insure favorable attitudes
toward the company. Top management is keenly aware of the importance of favorable employee, community, and general public opinion to
the continued success of its operations. The broad program is developed
on the principle that good employee relations are conducive to good
public relations, and that good public relations help to make better employee relations.

The channels of communication between the management of Johnson
& Johnson and its employees include direct person-to-person contacts
and a wide variety of printed media. The channels between management
and supervisors and union are predominantly through personal contact.
The importance of transmitting information, accurately and fully, to
staff or employees immediately under them is impressed upon all supervisors. The dissemination of information ranks high among the activities of the personnel department. In fact, three out of nine formal objectives of the personnel department are as follows:

"1. To insure the company's good standing with the public.
"2. To train and inform fully, and to release all additional latent
abilities and powers of our employees.
"3. To inspire and to solicit cooperation of the employees and to bridge
the gap between top management and employees by arriving at a
common understanding of worker and company attitudes, desires,
and needs. . . ."[1]

While these stated objectives indicate the company's interest in keeping
its employees informed on the aims, plans, and problems of management, it was considered important to the study to learn in more detail the
specific objectives in developing the communications program. The more
detailed picture was gained through interviews with four of the company's top executives, the chairman of the board, the president, the vice
president, and the director of personnel. Each one of these officers was
asked to express his views as to what information he considered to be
most important for the company to communicate to its employees.

[1] From *Personnel Department Organization.*

The chairman of the board regards the problem of communications in its broadest terms. In his opinion, the survival of our present economic system depends on the existence of teamwork among those whose efforts make the system function. The essence of teamwork is mutual confidence, which, in turn, is founded upon the exchange of trustworthy information. Thus, the chairman emphasized, management must share information with its employees not only to stimulate efficiency but also to safeguard the continuance of the system of free enterprise. Modern industry must become an educational as well as a business institution if it is to survive. Moreover, his concept of industrial education includes training that helps adjust the worker to his community life as well as to his job.

These objectives of the chairman of the board form the broad base for the company's informational program. The other executives interviewed added comments on specific matters that they believed to be important in management-employee communications. These executives were primarily concerned with the need for the proper application of policies to the rank and file. They were conscious of the fact that policies, formulated by top management, may not always seem necessary or logical to the employees unless the policies and the changes resulting from them are carefully explained in advance of their application. While it was recognized that an explanation alone might not eliminate employee discontent, it was felt that giving employees advance information regarding changes was essential to satisfactory management-employee relations.

The Johnson & Johnson management also wants its employees to have some understanding of the general problems of business management. In particular, these executives expressed a desire to develop an appreciation of simple economics and a "cost-consciousness" among the employees. Insofar as possible, management would like every employee to understand the relation between production costs and prices, and between prices and the ability of the company to maintain its sales and employment. In the words of one executive:

"We would like our employees to know that it is the housewife who sets the price for our products. . . . Production costs must be held at a level that will enable management to price its products so as to produce a maximum volume of sales; otherwise, both management and employees will lose."

In the opinion of another of these executives, it is the responsibility of management not only to give employees a positive concept of business economics, but also to use its communications system to counteract unfavorable propaganda which employees receive from other sources. This more defensive objective of the communication program was considered important because of the disruptive effects on employee morale of statements disseminated by those seeking radical changes in the present economic and political systems. Management, this executive believed, must make its voice heard in order to correct the impressions created by what it considers to be distorted facts and irresponsible allegations. Closely allied to the use of the informational program as a counter-propaganda measure is its use in preventing the spread of false rumors. While it is recognized that rumors are inevitable in any human organization, the Johnson & Johnson management wants to make certain that their employees have sufficient explicit information about company affairs to prevent the spread of false rumors.

Although management considered one important aim of its informational media to be to counteract certain propaganda, the top executives who were interviewed in no way regarded the employee communications program as a means of undermining the power or prestige of the union. On the contrary, top management at Johnson & Johnson seemed eager to share information with union leaders, and to use the informational program to help maintain harmonious labor relations and to add to the prestige of the local union. One of the executives in particular showed a keen awareness of the union's value as a channel of communication between management and employees, and all of the management representatives acknowledged the value of the union in this respect. Nevertheless, management expressed a uniform desire to strengthen its direct channels of communication with the employees and not to rely exclusively on the union.

B. Communications between Top Management and Supervisors

In studying employee and supervisory attitudes towards the existing informational program and channels of communication, it was evident that past as well as present conditions affected these attitudes. A change, for example, had been made in 1944 in the organization of the production department of the New Brunswick plant. Prior to this date, the department had, in effect, two executives responsible for its operation. In 1944, a single executive was placed in charge of manufacturing operations and a general reorganization of the supervisory organization followed. This change of itself was felt to have improved considerably the transmission of information from one level of management to another.

In 1947, the manufacturing operations of the New Brunswick plant headed up to the vice president of the manufacturing division to whom the superintendents of each of the three mills reported. The supervisory organization in the three mills (the gauze mill, the cotton mill, and the plaster mill) was similar. Reporting to the superintendent of the gauze mill were three foremen, each of whom was held responsible for one phase of its productive operations. Reporting to these foremen were assistant foremen, either responsible for a smaller segment of the department's operations or acting as shift foremen in the case of operations on more than one shift. Below the assistant foremen were group leaders, who were considered a part of management. As mentioned earlier, the positions of foremen and of lower levels of supervisors at Johnson & Johnson carry both prestige and responsibility for results.

1. *Methods for keeping supervisors informed*

Interviews with 26 supervisors below the level of superintendent indicated that the 1944 reorganization, with its resultant clarification of lines of authority and responsibility, contributed greatly to the functioning of the communication system from top management to lower supervision. The reorganization was accompanied by several other developments that improved supervisory communications. The newly appointed vice president of manufacturing, for example, began to hold regular weekly meetings with his superintendents. These weekly meetings have become an important link in the communications system. Proposed plans and policies and operating conditions are discussed informally, and all participants are allowed time and freedom to express their views at the regular Tuesday morning meeting. Each department head is expected to hold a similar meeting with his own staff on Tuesday afternoon or Wednesday, and to pass along the gist of the Tuesday morning discussion. Each foreman, in turn, is supposed to carry the information down the organizational chain to the assistant foremen and group leaders. If the information is to be given to all employees, a notice is placed on the bulletin boards or the employees are assembled as a group and an explanation made verbally by the supervisor in charge.

At the same time that the manufacturing division was reorganized, the personnel department was making noticeable progress in developing its supervisory training program. Originally designed to train candidates for supervisory positions during the wartime manpower shortage, the program was expanded to provide training for those already employed as supervisors.

The stated objectives of the supervisory training program include the following:

"To give supervisors a broader understanding of Johnson & Johnson business with the object of arousing their interest and stimulating their initiative in their work.

"To acquaint supervisors with the problems of management."

The training offered now includes a wide range of conferences dealing with the organization, functions, and problems of management as well as courses in technical subjects. A number of the conferences help directly to increase the supervisor's knowledge and understanding of company policies and procedures. A description of the conference on "Company Rules, Regulations and Services" states, for example:

"Part of the total training program at J & J is the formal induction of new employees. So that supervisors may have a better understanding of the objectives of the induction program, this conference presents in a condensed fashion the material of the regular orientation class. It has been interesting to discover how many supervisors from all levels have an incomplete knowledge of the policies and practices of the company for which they are working. They, above all, should have a comprehensive knowledge of the company."

All in all, management feels that the training conferences have proved their value as media for conveying information on company policies and for improving the supervisor's understanding of the broader problems of company operations. An important adjunct to the conference training program is a manual of standard practices prepared by the personnel department and available to every supervisor. This manual gives a concisely written description of all personnel policies and procedures.

An independent social organization of Johnson & Johnson foremen, the Supervisors Club, has, at times, served as a means of communication. Various representatives of higher management have given talks at the monthly meetings of the Club, and other less formal contacts are maintained.

2. Supervisory attitudes

Two main objectives were considered in interviewing supervisors of the New Brunswick plant. First, the questions aimed to find out how the supervisors felt toward the information they received from management and the way it was given to them. Second, in recognition of their vital role in communicating with the worker, supervisors were also asked their opinion regarding the relative importance of their part in transmitting information to the employees as compared with other channels.

a. Attitude toward communications
from management

The supervisors appeared to be generally satisfied with the information given them by higher management. Clearly, the reorganization of the manufacturing division had resulted in substantial improvements. The response to one question in particular, when analyzed in relation to the length of service of the respondents, supports this conclusion.

Of the 26 supervisors interviewed, 16 had been employed for 5 years or longer. All but one of these 16 believed that they were receiving in 1947 more information about the company than when they were first employed. Of 10 foremen employed less than 5 years, 3 noted a similar improvement. None of the supervisors, regardless of their length of service, thought that the company was giving them less information than formerly.

Those who felt that communications had improved mentioned most frequently three developments that had helped to bring about the improvement. These were: (1) regularly scheduled supervisory meetings, (2) training and other activities of the personnel department, and (3) a "change in management attitude." In addition, one supervisor mentioned the presence of an outside union as a factor influencing management to give its supervisors more information.

Response to another question seems to substantiate the impression that most Johnson & Johnson supervisors were satisfied with the methods used by management to communicate with them. Asked to suggest means of improving communications, 15 out of 25 replied that they could offer no suggestions. Seven of the remaining 10 supervisors liked the idea of a special management newsletter, when it was mentioned by the interviewer. Additional supervisory training and more meetings were recommended by two. A question specifically concerning the subject of meetings revealed that 19 out of 25 supervisors were participating in regular meetings, and only 4 out of the 25 thought that more frequent meetings would be helpful.

While the majority of supervisors were satisfied with the information given them, the interviews revealed a few weaknesses in the communications system. One point on which there was apparent room for improvement was the timing of communications. Supervisors were asked whether they "always, usually, or sometimes" received information concerning changes to be made in operating conditions in sufficient time to notify the workers in advance of the change. Although almost half of the supervisors answered that they *always* received information in plenty of time, a third of the group indicated that they were *usually* notified in sufficient time, and five individuals replied that the information was only *sometimes* available soon enough. It may be concluded from these replies that a substantial minority of supervisors felt that the improved timing of communications would help them fulfill more satisfactorily their own responsibility to keep the employee informed.

The most serious weakness in management communications appeared to be in the dissemination of information concerning union relations. Ten of the 26 supervisors felt that management had not made its attitude toward the union entirely clear, and the majority believed that shop stewards were better informed about labor negotiations than were supervisors. While it is possible that the supervisors' thinking on this point may have been colored by resentment against sharing some of their own functions with shop stewards, that does not lessen the foremen's feeling of inadequacy of information. Rather it suggests the need for careful study of means of improving intra-management communications on labor relations matters.

b. Attitude toward transmitting information

All of the supervisors interviewed believed that it was worthwhile for them to explain operating and policy changes to their employees. Nevertheless a majority were of the opinion that workers receive much of their information about the company from other sources than supervision. This attitude was revealed in the responses to two questions. Asked to mention the principal sources of employee information on changes in company policies, the supervisors ranked the bulletin board first. However, 16 added that the workers also heard of these changes through their supervisors. Other sources mentioned were the union stewards and rumor. A second question relevant to this point was:

> "As things are now, do you think that wage employees find out more about the company's problems from their supervisors, from company pamphlets and newspapers, through the union, or how?"

Ten of the 26 foremen mentioned supervision as the chief source of employee information, but 12 mentioned the union and 7 the bulletin board. Company newspapers and pamphlets were believed to be of minor importance. Other sources of information again included rumor as well as local newspapers. Apparently, experience had led the supervisors to believe that their employees looked elsewhere for much of their information. To what extent this attitude affected the supervisor's efforts to disseminate information, the survey did not disclose.

C. Management-Union Communications

1. *At the top level*

Leaders of management and union in the New Brunswick plant agreed that they had achieved a peaceful relationship between 1944 when the union was recognized as the bargaining agent and 1947. It is apparent that the growth of such a relationship requires a constructive approach by both sides. Interviews with management and union officers indicated that, for the most part, an attitude of mutual trust and confidence prevailed. Such mutual confidence might not exist if top management was unwilling to share information with the union officers, or if either side was unwilling to listen with respect to the other. Although the union officers expressed some reservations in their generally favorable opinion of Johnson & Johnson's labor policies, these officers meet with company officers on an extremely friendly basis.

Although, by 1947, grievances were occurring with less and less frequency, union and management representatives met weekly whether or not there were specific grievances to be settled. Moreover, the door of the chairman of the board was always open to the union representatives who, on more than one occasion, had used this means of assuring themselves that their side of the story was heard. Management also was willing to cooperate with union representatives at the national level, insofar as their questions involved the Johnson & Johnson plants organized by the Textile Workers.

There were, however, two factors in the union-management relationship at Johnson & Johnson that may have interfered with the free interchange of information between the two parties. One important weakness in the relationship felt by the union was what might be termed the "dilemma of paternalism."[1] The union believed that the company's pre-unionization paternalism still existed to some extent. The comprehensive personnel program created a fear in the minds of the union leaders that the net effect of the program would be to reduce the employees' interest in and loyalty to the union.

Another dissatisfaction on the part of the union resulted from the fact that some of the Johnson & Johnson plants were non-union or were organized by a different union. This second problem might be termed the "dilemma of decentralization." By 1947, the question was being raised frequently as to how far top management could follow its general policy of decentralization where labor relations were concerned. In the company's plants located in the South, union officials were convinced

[1] See also Chapter V, p. 47.

that local management had openly resisted their organization drives. These circumstances and the existence of the two company plants in the New Brunswick area outside the T.W.U.A. bargaining unit led to resentment among the New Brunswick union officials. Although management protested its lack of control over decentralized plants, the union apparently was not fully convinced and, furthermore, began to fear that its acceptance in New Brunswick might be only on a temporary basis.

Thus, while the company executives increasingly recognized the importance of sharing information about the company with the union, they were also beginning to realize that these fears on the part of the union were affecting the value of the union as an agent in promoting the downward flow of information to the workers. A problem facing management in 1947 was how to overcome the doubts of the union's leaders and reconcile decentralized labor policies and an aggressive personnel program with collective bargaining.

2. *At the shop level*

Top management and lower supervision were virtually unanimous in believing that the union had assisted management in communicating with the production workers. As might be expected, however, the actual extent to which different supervisors accepted the principle of dealing on a friendly basis with a union varied considerably. One department superintendent, for example, stated that the organization of his employees by the C.I.O. was "the greatest thing that ever happened to them." According to the union, another superintendent was "only waiting for a sign from top management to crack down." While both of these attitudes were probably exaggerated, they do give some indication of the problems involved in seeking to gain management-wide acceptance of a policy adopted at the top level.

Below the level of department superintendent, most of the plant supervisors apparently recognized the importance of the shop steward as a channel of communication with the rank and file. In all but three instances, the foremen interviewed said that they notified the shop steward first in announcing changes in policy. Interviews with 15 shop stewards lent support to the statements of supervisors that shop stewards were advised of changes before general announcements were made to the employees. However, although 11 of the 15 union stewards said that they heard of changes before other employees, only 6 of the 11 said that they received the information through their foremen. The remaining five first heard of changes through the union.

The response to another question asked of shop stewards does not indicate a specific defect in supervisory-shop steward communications, but rather reflects inconsistencies in managerial attitudes that affect these communications. As reported in the previous section, almost all the supervisors questioned believed that management had clearly advised them regarding its policy toward the union. But, if this policy was clearly *understood* by lower supervision, it apparently had not been *effectuated* in such a way as to remove all doubts from the minds of the shop stewards.

Twenty-four foremen were asked which, if either, of the following statements of policy more nearly described management's attitude toward the union:

"A. Treat the union fairly, but deal with it no more than is necessary under the terms of the labor agreement.
"B. Treat the union fairly, and seek its support in all matters affecting employees even when the union's support is not required under the terms of the labor agreement."

Their replies showed a very high degree of common understanding of company policy. One of the group chose "A," 21 chose "B," and only 2 chose neither. One of these two was "not sure" and the other interpreted management's policy to be to "treat the union fairly but don't let it walk over you."

Thirteen shop stewards were asked which of the same two statements more nearly described the attitude of their foremen. Their replies showed considerably less agreement as to the attitudes revealed in supervisory action. Three of the stewards felt that "A" was more descriptive of their foreman's attitude, five chose "B," and five agreed with neither statement. Of the five in the last group, four felt their foremen were not entirely fair and the fifth that the assistant foreman was fair but that the foreman resented collective bargaining.

The shop stewards were also asked whether or not they thought the attitude of their supervisors was the same as the attitude of top management regarding the union. Of the 13 stewards who had replied to the first question, only three expressed the belief that supervisory and top management attitudes toward the union were alike. Four of the stewards expressed no opinion, and six said that top management and supervisory attitudes differed. In most cases, the opinion was that top management was more cooperative towards the union than were the line supervisors.

IV. MANAGEMENT-EMPLOYEE COMMUNICATIONS

A. MEANS OF KEEPING EMPLOYEES INFORMED

1. *Through the line organization*

The top management of Johnson & Johnson showed full awareness of the importance of the line organization as a direct channel of communication. The chain of command, from the vice president of manufacturing through the foreman to his assistants and to the employee, is accepted as the chief conduit of the management's system of communications in regard to operating instructions and the daily maintenance of safety and discipline.

The weekly meeting of the plant superintendents with the vice president of manufacturing is the heart of the present system of line communications. While emphasis is given to the need of getting information intended for the employees to them as quickly and as accurately as possible, in most cases it is left to the superintendents and foremen how best to accomplish this. If the information is of a routine nature, it may be put into a memorandum and posted on the bulletin board. More important announcements may be given directly to individual employees by the foreman or through a departmental meeting. When, for example, in June, 1947, it was necessary to shut down the New Brunswick plant for one week because of over-stocked inventories, many department superintendents called their employees together and personally explained the situation to them.

Interviews with management and the poll of employees[1] showed a higher regard both among top management and among the workers for the supervisor's role in communications than the supervisors accepted for themselves.[2] Management has attempted to develop its supervisors in this respect and has succeeded at least to the degree that employees believe that improved communications are in part due to improved supervision.[3] It was apparent that the foremen were an effective part of the communications system, even though management has yet to convince them of their outstanding importance in keeping the workers informed.

[1] See Tables 4, 5, and 6, pp. 39-40.
[2] See p. 35, for comment on supervisory attitudes.
[3] Table 1, p. 34.

2. *Through printed media*

Johnson & Johnson distributes a wide variety of written material to its employees, including a semi-monthly newspaper, an employee handbook, and occasional reprints of articles written by the chairman of the board. Booklets describing such specific company plans as the suggestion system and the group insurance plan are also distributed. The employee newspaper, the *J & J Bulletin*, and the employee handbook, *Our Job at Johnson & Johnson*, are worthy of special mention from the standpoint of make-up, style, and attractiveness.

The *Bulletin* features a variety of good photographs focused on the worker rather than on the machinery and process of production. The employee handbook, first published in 1945, also includes a large number of photographs and sketches. Prominent items in this publication are letters to employees signed by the chairman of the board and the president of the company. In addition, the handbook includes a diagrammatic description of the manufacturing process, and sections entitled "Our responsibilities at J & J" and "Our privileges at J & J." The former refers to disciplinary rules and procedures, and the latter refers to the company's personnel, training, and recreational programs. These publications are distributed through the foremen, and are also available at the receptionist's desk in the personnel department.

Bulletin boards are strategically placed in every department's lunch room. All material to be posted is distributed to the foremen who are responsible for posting. However, a representative of the personnel department also makes a weekly tour of inspection of the bulletin boards.

3. *Through the training program*

In 1944 when the industrial engineering department was decentralized, the emphasis in the company's employee relations program shifted from industrial engineering to a program stressing the improvement of human relations. A training director joined the personnel department in 1944 and, between this year and 1947, the activities of the training department were progressively expanded.

The growth of the training department at Johnson & Johnson was predicated upon a long-run point of view that human relations can be significantly (and profitably) improved by means of training and education. The ultimate objective of the training program is to develop a constructive attitude on the part of the employee towards his job and the company. In fulfilling this objective, the training staff believes that any information that will aid the employee in adjusting himself to his job, to his company, and to his community is a proper subject for employee training. Training courses at New Brunswick and Ethicon Suture have included such diversified subjects as public speaking, social hygiene, civics, economics, and fire fighting, as well as supervisory and operator training. A comprehensive orientation course is given to all new employees and to some of the old employees.

Specifically, the training program has sought to disseminate information regarding:

(1) *Facts*, such as company rules and regulations, insurance, and seniority.
(2) *Attitudes*, or feelings, such as pride in the company's products, confidence in management, and the company's respect for long-service employees.
(3) *Skills*, such as a machine or trade skill, safety, and fire prevention.

In 1946, a total of 540 employees had participated in the training program; in 1947, the number had increased to 1085.[1] In addition to the special courses, the training staff spends as much time assisting the line departments in situations in which training can be of help, such as the application of new policies and practices.

Johnson & Johnson's training program has not, however, reached the final phase of its planned development. Many workers have as yet taken no part in the training program. Preliminary to the future extension of the training program to all employees, an "Educational Conference Committee" was formed in 1947. The Committee consisted of three union members, including the president of the local union, the plant steward, and the educational director of the Joint Board; two members chosen from the company's office staff, and a representative of the training department. The Committee met twice a week for an hour and a half on company time and discussed such subjects as the history of the company, management policies, elementary economics, public speaking, and writing. Full participation in the discussion was encouraged, and, towards the end of the course, each participant prepared a written statement of the policies that he believed should be followed in order to obtain good employee relations. Each statement was then discussed, point by point, until unanimous agreement was reached. It was planned to summarize these statements in a booklet signed by all the members of the Conference Committee and to distribute copies to all employees.

[1] These totals are for the full years, 1946 and 1947.

4. *Other media*

a. Open House

April, 1947, marked the sixtieth anniversary of Johnson & Johnson. The occasion was commemorated by an Open House to which were invited employees, their families and friends, and the general public. Besides commemorating the anniversary, the main purpose of the Open House was to improve the prestige of the company in the eyes of the public, particularly in the New Brunswick community. At the same time, the Open House, which was operated for two weeks, gave additional information about the company to its employees.

The Open House featured exhibits, photographs and demonstrations of the company's products, plants, and machinery, as well as conducted tours through the New Brunswick mill. As many as 2000 visitors were entertained each day. Each of the exhibits stressed the importance that the company attaches to maintaining good personnel relations, and each exhibit was manned by an employee from the production line of the product being displayed. The personnel department's exhibit was located in the most prominent position on the floor. An "Old-Timer's" booth was operated with the help of retired employees who greeted their friends among the guests and talked with the general public. A booklet describing the company and its history and products was distributed to all who attended.

b. Plant broadcasting system

The in-plant broadcasting system is used extensively at the Ethicon Suture plant to disseminate management information. In this plant, for example, a series of "soap opera" skits had been developed and proved effective in securing employee cooperation. As a result of one of these plant radio programs, in which the parts were assigned to various employees, glass breakage at this plant was decreased by 48 per cent in six weeks.

c. Miscellaneous

Frequent press releases prepared for the New Brunswick newspapers are intended primarily for public relations but are also a source of information for the company's employees.

Other methods of communication between management and worker undoubtedly exist in Johnson & Johnson. The "grapevine" must, of course, be taken for granted in any human organization, even when management's aim is to get accurate information to employees so timed as to reduce rumor to a minimum.

B. Employee Attitudes Towards the Informational Program

In order to evaluate the methods used at Johnson & Johnson in transmitting information to the employees, a questionnaire-poll of 359 production workers was conducted. The results of the poll afford an illuminating insight into the actual operation of the communications system. In evaluating the responses, it is sometimes impossible to distinguish between management channels and union channels of communication since the worker is the focal point of both. This difficulty, however, serves only to emphasize the fact that, under favorable conditions, management and union supplement each other in their efforts to keep the worker informed.

1. *Regarding the availability of information from the company*

The poll of 359 employees in 1947 showed definitely that changes in plant organization, the establishment of a personnel department, and unionization, all occurring after 1940, had had a marked influence on the attitude of workers in regard to the company's willingness to share information with them. More than half (56 per cent) of the production workers polled were of the opinion that they received more information at the time of the poll (July and August, 1947) than when they were first employed. Of the respondents with more than five years' service, two-thirds believed that they were kept better informed about company affairs in 1947 than in the earlier years of their employment.

Those who felt that they were comparatively better informed about company affairs were asked: "What changes since you first started to work here have resulted in your being better informed?" Thirty-six per cent of these employees said either that they were not sure exactly

TABLE 1. CONDITIONS FELT TO HAVE RESULTED IN IMPROVED
MANAGEMENT-WORKER COMMUNICATIONS

Response	*Per cent responding**
Union organization and collective bargaining	33
Improved supervisory management	22
More information on bulletin board	13
Company publications	10
Increased personal interest of the employee	8
Fellow workers more cooperative	4
Public address system	5
Other conditions	6

* A few workers mentioned more than one condition.

why they felt better informed or they made no reply to the question. Table I refers to the responses of the 64 per cent who mentioned a specific change or changes that had resulted in improved communications.

In interpreting the above table, it should be recognized that judgment had to be used in the classification of some replies. Thus the table provides only an approximation of the relative value placed on developments that had, in the workers' opinion, resulted in their being given more information. For example, unionization and improved supervision as well as unknown personal factors may have given the individual employees, whose responses are put in the category "Increased personal interest," a greater sense of personal responsibility for keeping themselves informed. Such comments as "Times have changed," "Now I don't hesitate to ask," and "Not working under such tense feeling" were even harder to classify and had to be lumped under "Other conditions." It should also be remembered, in attempting to weigh one influence against another, that a number of the changes referred to by the employees occurred at about the same time and were closely interrelated.

Two aspects of the response to this question are particularly worthy of note. It is significant that one-third of those naming a specific reason for the improvement in communications referred to the union. This would seem to indicate unmistakably that, whether or not the union was the chief factor, its presence promoted the feeling among employees that more information was given to them or that it was more readily obtainable on request.

The importance of the supervisor in the chain of communications is also highlighted. What the employees think of the supervisors' willingness or unwillingness to give them information was revealed by responses to other questions. Asked, "How easy or difficult is it for you to see your foreman if you wish to have a talk with him?", 72 per cent of the employees replied "Easy," 23 per cent "Sometimes difficult," and 1 per cent "Almost impossible." Four per cent failed to reply. Asked "When you talk with your foreman, how willing is he to explain things which interest you most?", 72 per cent replied "Always willing," 18 per cent "Sometimes willing," 5 per cent "Not very willing." Five per cent indicated they didn't know or failed to respond. These responses show a high degree of employee satisfaction with their supervisor's willingness to give them information. The 23 per cent who were felt to be "sometimes difficult" to see or only "sometimes willing" or "not very willing to explain things" might be viewed as a rough

measure of the need for improvement in supervision in an effort to develop more satisfactory communications.

2. *Regarding specific media*

a. Company publications

Answers to a number of questions in the employee poll as well as
interviews with supervisors suggested that written media were ranked
considerably lower than verbal communications. Answers to other questions, however, showed a real interest in the company's periodical and
pamphlet publications. The extent to which these publications are read
is indicated by the following tabulation of responses:

TABLE 2. EXTENT TO WHICH COMPANY LITERATURE IS READ

	Per cent responding	
Continuing publications	*Sometimes read*	*Read nearly every issue*
Company magazine	91	83
Articles by Chairman of Board	56	31
(Daily newspapers)	81	79
Pamphlets	*Have read at least once*	*Has been most useful*
Employee handbook	42	16
Suggestion system booklet	37	6
Group insurance booklet	45	16

The response, even allowing for some over-credit on the reading
side, shows that the *J & J Bulletin* is read by a large majority of the
employees. While much of the *Bulletin* is devoted to personal news
items, each issue contains some information about the company and its
policies and products. However much or little time the employees give
to the articles dealing with the company, management can at least be
sure that it is presenting its story in a popular medium. The interest
shown in the reprints of articles by the chairman of the board, although
considerably less than in the *Bulletin*, is also high enough to make these
articles a worthwhile channel of getting the chief executive's ideas to
the employees.

The comparatively low reader interest in special pamphlets revealed
by this question agrees with the response to a few other questions in
showing that employees prefer to depend on their supervisor, shop
steward, or the personnel department for information on specific
activities.

b. The training program

When the survey of Johnson & Johnson workers was made, the company's training program was in the process of being expanded to offer instruction to the rank and file similar to that which had been given supervisory employees. Only about one-fourth of the production workers polled had participated in any part of the training program. Moreover, most of the instruction that they had received was given for the purpose of developing occupational skills or, in the orientation course, for the purpose of disseminating factual information concerning company policies. Regardless of the specific purpose of the training course, however, instructors had attempted to treat every subject in such a way as to develop a favorable attitude on the part of the employees toward the company.

Although none of the employees (see Table 1) referred to the training program among the "changed conditions" helping them to receive more information about the company, response to several other questions indicates that this program may have been a direct influence in promoting an understanding of the company's problems. (It was undoubtedly an important influence in improving the quality of supervision, which, as was seen above, counted heavily with the employees.) For example, in responding to the question asking whether they felt that they received more or less information since they first started to work for Johnson & Johnson, 70 per cent of those employees who had received training felt better informed, as compared with only slightly more than half of those who had not been exposed to the training program.

Along with many other companies at the close of the war, the management of Johnson & Johnson carried on an intensive campaign to reduce the costs of production in order to maintain their competitive position in the post-war economy. The company used the supervisors, the company magazine, and the training program to develop a sense of "cost-consciousness" among the employees. Management stressed the fact that, while cost reduction would benefit the company, it would also benefit the worker in terms of greater job security and more jobs. The extent to which this idea was accepted by the rank and file is illustrated by the response to the following question. Workers were asked: "Do you think that producing things at lower costs helps to make your job more secure, or do lower costs only make more money for the company without benefiting you?" More than half of the workers indicated by their response that their attitude coincided with that of management; approximately 10 per cent said that cost reductions would only make more money for the company; and 18 per cent were not sure who would benefit if costs were cut. A further analysis of the responses that agreed with management's attitude on the basis of participation and non-participation in the training program indicated that 73 per cent of those who had received training felt that they would benefit from lowered costs, as compared with 52 per cent of those who had not participated in the training program.

3. *Regarding the adequacy of information on certain subjects*

a. Changes in operating conditions

Several questions were asked concerning the transmission of information having a direct influence on the worker's job or shop conditions. The response to the first group of these questions is particularly interesting in that management had taken great pains to disseminate information of this nature just prior to the time the poll was made. In the summer of 1947, the company discovered that actual demand for the products of its New Brunswick plant was considerably below production estimates that had been forecast earlier in the year and that inventories were too high. Up to this time, many employees in the New Brunswick mill had been working overtime and production on most machines had been held to the wartime level. Top management felt the need for an immediate change in production policies, but was also sensitive to the difficulty of explaining this shift in policy without arousing a sense of insecurity on the part of the employees.

Meetings were held almost simultaneously with departmental superintendents and top union representatives in order to advise them of the situation. Several alternative solutions were discussed, and the union tentatively agreed to support a policy whereby some employees would be temporarily laid off and the mill would continue its operations on a reduced schedule. However, when the union leaders proposed this plan to their members at a mass meeting, the rank and file voted for a week's shutdown for all rather than "overtime for a few." Management agreed to adopt this second policy and, shortly thereafter, notices to all employees were posted on the departmental bulletin boards. In several departments, the superintendents called their employees together to explain the reasons for the shutdown and to alleviate their fears. Shop stewards, in most cases, were notified of the decision prior to the general announcement.

Employees were polled within two weeks after they had returned from the layoff. One question sought to ascertain whether or not they felt that they had been informed in advance of the reasons why changes in operating conditions were necessary. The response to this question was as follows:

TABLE 3. ADVANCE INFORMATION ON CHANGES IN THE SHOP

Question: When changes are made in the hours and working conditions in your department, are you informed in advance *why* these changes are necessary?

Response	Per cent
Yes	71
No	20
Don't know	3
No response	6

Apparently something over one-fifth of the workers felt that they received inadequate information in advance of the change in spite of the effort made to inform them.

The response to two related questions reveals the difference between the sources from which workers receive notification of change and the source from which an explanation would be sought if more information was desired. The data in Table 4 refer to 83 per cent of those polled who mentioned one or more specific sources of notification of change in operating conditions. Table 5 is an analysis of the 75 per cent who gave some specific source from which they would seek a fuller explanation.

TABLE 4. SOURCE OF NOTIFICATION OF CHANGE

Question: How are you notified about these changes?

Response	Per cent responding
Supervision	48
Bulletin board	28
Shop steward	3 ⎫ 13
Shop steward and supervision	10 ⎭
Public address system	7
Fellow workers and others	4

TABLE 5. WHERE EMPLOYEES SEEK INFORMATION ON CHANGES

Question: If you wanted to find out exactly how these shop changes may affect your job, what would you do?

Response	Per cent responding
Ask supervision	49
Ask shop stewards	34 ⎫ 49
Ask shop stewards or supervision	15 ⎭
Other	2

The principal contrast between the replies to these two questions is in
the number who receive notification from their shop steward and the
much larger number who would go to him for an explanation of the
effect of the change on the individual job. This inclination to seek explanation through the shop steward was further substantiated by the
responses of employees when given an opportunity to suggest improved
channels of communication.[1]

b. Wage determination

Another battery of questions concerned the dissemination of information regarding methods for setting wage rates and establishing work
loads. In this case, top management had made no particular effort to
see that its employees were informed. Union representatives, however,
had complete information regarding job classification and the methods
for setting piece and incentive rates.

The extent of employee desire for more information on wage determination was indicated by replies to the question, "Do you need more
information about the method for setting your wage rate and work
load?" All but eight per cent of the group gave some response to this
question; 41 per cent said "Yes," 49 per cent "No," and 2 per cent
"Don't care." Asked "Who, if anyone, has been most helpful in explaining how your wages are figured?", 45 per cent of the total polled
failed to respond or said no one had been helpful. The 55 per cent who
felt that someone had been helpful in explaining how their rates were
set mentioned the following:

TABLE 6. SOURCE OF EXPLANATION OF WAGE DETERMINATION

Response	Per cent responding
Supervision	54
Union	29
Fellow workers and others	13
Time study man	4

It is interesting to note in this that while the number who had been
helped by a member of supervision was only slightly higher than the
number (Table 4) thus notified of a change in operation, the union
apparently played a much more active role in getting wage information
to employees.

c.   Insurance and other benefits

Several questions in the survey dealt with subjects that, while not
directly affecting the worker on his job, are closely related to the work-

---

[1] See Table 9, p. 42.

er's personal interests. Response to one of these questions reflects the role of the company's personnel department as administrator of the group insurance plans. Asked where they could find out just what types of insurance were available, the employees mentioned the following sources:

TABLE 7. INFORMATION REGARDING GROUP INSURANCE

Response	Per cent responding*
Personnel department	59
Supervision	11
Union	7
Insurance booklet or policy	6
Fellow workers	3
Don't know or no response	22

* Some respondents mentioned more than one source.

Although, as indicated by this response, the channel of communication used to secure information regarding group insurance is predominantly the personnel staff rather than the line supervision, it is evident that person-to-person contact is overwhelmingly preferred to the printed booklet which is distributed by the personnel department.

In May, 1947, the company, in conjunction with the union, made arrangements with a local bank for workers to secure personal loans at a reasonable interest rate. Information concerning the new loan plan was passed down through the organizational chain of command, and notices were distributed by the personnel department for posting on all bulletin boards. The union did not take a very active part in publicizing the plan; and, except in a few departments where bank identification cards were distributed to all employees, supervisory management relied almost entirely on the bulletin board or public address system to announce the new loan plan. According to the questionnaire response, almost two-thirds of the workers had been informed of the plan. Those who said they were notified indicated the following sources for this information:

TABLE 8. SOURCES OF INFORMATION ON LOAN PLAN

Response	Per cent responding*
Bulletin board	58
Received identification card	15
Fellow workers and others	10
Public address system	5
No specific source mentioned	22

* Some respondents mentioned more than one source.

The favorable response to this question was high, but some criticism of management's too great reliance on the bulletin board to get information to employees was made by a number who did not know of the plan. Some commented: "It was posted in the lunchroom but many people eat outside and few saw it personally," and "I didn't know about it until I read this question and I *don't* think that is good management."

Reviewing the response to all questions whose subject was directly related to the personal or job interests of the worker, it is clear that employees depend primarily on their immediate supervisors and the shop stewards to keep them informed. Another point that stands out is that, in spite of the efforts made to get important information to all employees, from 29 to 45 per cent of those polled either were too uncertain of the source of a particular type of information to respond or felt that they had not received the information.

4. *Suggestions for improving communications*

Two questions provided the employees with an opportunity for making suggestions as to how management could improve communications. One of these dealt with the media of communications; the other with the substance of communications. The response, in both instances, may indicate possible weaknesses in the management-employee communications system.

The question regarding the channels of communication offered the respondents a choice of eight suggestions for improving communications. The workers were asked to check those suggestions which they favored. Of the 89 per cent of the workers responding, most of them checked more than one item with the following results:

TABLE 9. SUGGESTIONS ON METHODS

Question: If the company wants to keep you better informed, which of the following suggestions do you think would be helpful?

Suggestion	Per cent responding
Meetings at which department superintendents could explain new policies	18
Meetings at which department superintendents *and* union officers could explain new policies	34
More training courses	12
Letters to every employee explaining new plans and policies	18
More information on the bulletin boards	36
Announcements over the plant loudspeaker system	25
Encourage foremen to give out more information	33
Give more information to the union officers and let them tell the employees about it	33

Following the check list, space was provided for additional suggestions. A few criticisms were made, such as, "No time to read the bulletin board," and "When they inform us, I hope it's everyone, not just a few." Several constructive suggestions were also made. These were: "Have a 'rumor delegate' whose job it would be to hear rumors and report them to management"; "Hold semi-monthly meetings with both labor and management in on them"; "There is not enough time to read the mountains of literature bestowed on us—*make it simple.*"

Several conclusions may be made from a study of these responses. Aside from the bulletin board, which is apparently accepted as a convenient channel of communications, the most popular media that were mentioned all favor verbal communications as against written communications. A third of the respondents thought that management should encourage foremen to give out more information. While only 18 per cent thought that meetings in which department superintendents alone would explain new policies would be helpful, 34 per cent approved of the idea of such meetings if union officers and department superintendents together were to explain policies. Similarly, a third of the employees believed that management should "give more information to the union officers and let them tell the employees about it." The employees generally want the people to whom they feel free to talk to know the answers to their questions and to keep them informed, and they would like the union to participate in an explanation of changes whether the communication is on an individual or group basis.

The second question sought to determine what types of information workers would like to have from the company. The employees were asked: "If you could have a talk with the president of Johnson & Johnson, what questions, if any, would you want to ask him?" Fifty-eight per cent of the group did not reply. The response of the remaining 42 per cent is shown in Table 10.

The lack of response as well as some of the responses to this question suggest either that the majority of employees found it hard to think of asking the president of the company for information or felt no particular need for further information. Several stated, "I'd be afraid to talk," or "Lots of questions, but I'd forget them all." The more definite replies indicate that what most frequently came to mind first was some general or personal grievance or a subject related to the employee's personal welfare. The five per cent interested in more information on future operation schedules and the eight per cent interested in broader business and economic conditions may indicate how infrequently the employees recognize the direct relationship between the stability of the company

TABLE 10. SUGGESTED TOPICS OF DISCUSSION
WITH THE PRESIDENT OF THE COMPANY

Response	Per cent responding*
Relating to better wages or hours	19
Relating to wage inequalities	10
Relating to better working conditions and work materials	9
Relating to business or economic conditions	8
Relating to request for job transfer	7
Relating to future operation schedule and job security	5
Relating to failure of management to carry out announced policies	5
Personal remarks or miscellaneous	12
Not sure or no questions	26

* Some respondents mentioned more than one topic.

and their own welfare; or it may indicate that most workers are content to do their job in return for fair treatment and to leave the broader aspects of the business to management.

The 12 per cent of replies classified as "personal or miscellaneous" included in about equal parts requests on non-employment matters such as "to help the veterans get better housing"; questions of a highly skeptical or critical nature such as, "How would it be possible to see him if no satisfaction could be got from other sources?"; or favorable comments, such as, "I would like to compliment him on his 'pioneering' better labor-management relations and discuss it."

The responses to this last question of the poll reveal, perhaps more than any other, the handicaps management must overcome in developing a successful informational program. First of all, "actions speak louder than words," and management's statements of intent must not far outrun the ability of the first-line supervisors to fulfill the intent. Otherwise there is risk of many employees feeling as the few who would ask the president, "Why after spending all they do on 'Personnel,' do they not follow out their policies?"

Secondly there is the problem of the wide gap existing between top management and the workers revealed both by the failure of a large percentage of the group to respond to this question and by the types of subjects in which they indicated an interest. Also as was shown in response to the question regarding better channels of information,[1] workers prefer to receive information from their foremen or from the local union officers or stewards. To be equally interested in getting information from as high an authority as the superintendent, they would like to have a joint explanation of policies. Management's general policies

[1] See Table 9, p. 42.

and problems apparently have little reality and are of little interest to the employee except as they are related directly to his own work situation. In spite of these attitudes, however, it appears that Johnson & Johnson management is succeeding to some extent in presenting company financial data to employees in a way that is meaningful to them. This may be deduced from the following employee response to the statement-question, "The company recently distributed information about how it spends its income. Would you like to continue receiving this information?": Yes—66 per cent; No—8 per cent; Don't care—17 per cent; No response—9 per cent.

V. THE UNION'S INFORMATIONAL PROGRAM

A. PRINCIPAL OBJECTIVES

BOTH similarities and differences were found between the objectives of the Textile Workers Union in communicating with its membership and the objectives of Johnson & Johnson management in transmitting information to its employees. Observation of the worker on the job in his relationships to the company and the union suggests more similarity than difference. Study of the management's and the union's objectives in communications beyond the needs of the comparatively narrow job relationships reveal some similarities but also a number of fundamental differences.

Interviews with representatives of the union at the local, regional, and national level brought out the following principal aims in the Textile Workers efforts to maintain satisfactory communications with the members of Local 630.

1. *To keep all levels of the union and its members adequately informed on job or business issues, and acquainted with the functioning of a "business union."* Several union representatives pointed out the importance of considering communications as a two-way matter. This, they felt, was particularly the essence of communications at the worker-shop steward level. While there are many subjects on which the steward must give information to the worker, his job is primarily keeping in touch with the individual, answering his questions, settling grievances, and doing whatever is necessary to represent and help him. The emphasis on this link of the union's chain of communications is in part on having a well informed and efficient group of stewards, in part on developing throughout the membership an understanding of the function of the union in handling grievances and collective bargaining and, perhaps most strongly, on developing personal loyalty to the union.

In giving the worker information on job or business issues, union and management may agree on much of the information, and the shop stewards and foreman may be used as parallel or joint channels for announcements and explanations of job changes, wage rates, and similar matters. Different points of view may exist, however, in regard to "facts" that are involved in collective bargaining. Differences are even more likely to exist when the subject to be communicated is a matter of ideas rather than fact.

Thus, even in a situation with as friendly relationships as those between the officers of Local 630 and the management of Johnson & Johnson, the union tends to be on the alert in regard to any information from management to employees in which the union has not participated from the beginning. Union leaders, for instance, expressed some feeling of anxiety lest an extensive management personnel and informational program diminish the employees' loyalty to the union. These leaders were inclined to feel that, because management had the advantage in terms of financial ability and control of the workers' time in any contest involving the channeling of information, the union's contacts with its members should aim primarily to develop a sense of belonging to the group rather than to give them extensive information.

2. *To make the individual worker aware of his role and that of the local in the broader labor movement.* While the main task of Local 630 in its communications with its members was felt to be to weld them into a loyal group, participating in and supporting the union in day-to-day affairs and in any trial of strength between management and the union, the desire for developing a broader view of unionism among the members was also expressed by all of the leaders interviewed. This objective had several aspects.

In the first place, being a good union member involved not only knowledge of the organization and functions of the Textile Workers Union, but also participation in the activities of the local. Publications of the union can point out the democratic nature of the union, it was stated, but only participation in the government of the local and in its decisions can give the worker the sense of being a part of a democratic organization.

In the second place, the union leadership wished to develop some understanding of the extent to which the common welfare of workers might be affected by one bargaining situation. They would like their local members to have some information about and interest in the union's status and collective bargaining problems in the company as a whole and in the industry as well as in the plant.

A third aspect of the aim of the union's informational media in showing the individual worker that he was an important part of the labor movement was to point out to him and help him meet his responsibilities in the social and political activities of the union. This last point was considered essential if unions as a whole were to be effective representatives of their members in a democratic society and were also to give their members opportunities for satisfactory social expression. It was felt particularly that members must recognize and approve of these broader functions of their own union if they were "to lift their sights" higher than the immediate economic gains won through any specific collective bargaining situation. One leader, deploring what he called "slot-machine unionism" (where the members "put in their dues and expect to get a big raise"), felt that as the collective bargaining function of the union became well understood, the union's efforts must be given more to creating an interest in the history, philosophy, and social and political functions of unionism in a democratic society.

3. *To encourage wider participation of the union and its members in community activities.* This objective in union communications is closely related to the broader one above of gaining wide membership understanding of and participation in the labor movement as a whole. One of the Textile Workers officers in particular emphasized the value of union participation in community activities. It is his belief that such union participation is of benefit both to the community and to the union. It increases the prestige of the union in the eyes of its members and the public; it also helps to avoid an over-concentration on immediate economic objectives and to develop an interest in a community approach to social activities and to the solution of social problems.

4. *To help the individual member towards self-improvement.* The educational program of Local 630 is concerned not only with courses of vocational value, but also with courses that are principally of a cultural or recreational nature. As one union officer put it, the union must "always inculcate a desire for the better things of life."

The union representatives of the various levels agreed that the above points covered the principal objectives of intra-union communications. They also agreed that the first point—keeping the shop stewards and members informed on and interested in day-to-day union-management activities and issues and developing a sense of solidarity by "a kind of osmosis"—would probably remain the principal concern of local leaders. Opinions varied as to just how much the union's educational program, recreational activities, and participation in community affairs would influence the individual worker's loyalty to the union and the efficient functioning of the local. The leaders all saw the need, however, of developing a broad understanding of unionism among the membership if economic issues are to be settled with a minimum of conflict and if the union and the individual workers are to be effective instruments in the maintenance of a democratic society. But they also recognize that the worker's chief interests are in his personal and job situations. The broader objectives of the union, it is felt, can be attained only as the members attain a better understanding of the relationship of the broader goals to the specific situation, and gain individual satisfaction from participating in union activities.

B.   Methods Used in Keeping its Membership Informed

1. *Meetings*

If every member of Local 630 participated in union meetings, the problem of intra-union communication would be reduced appreciably. The Textile Workers' organization facilitates the transmission of ideas upwards and downwards by means of meetings. The constitution of Local 630 requires it to hold membership meetings at least once a month. The Executive Board, consisting of shop stewards and union officers, also meets once a month, and the local officers meet weekly with the officers of the Joint Board to carry on the routine business of running the union. Representatives of each local meet monthly as the Joint Board's Executive Committee. Delegates are elected to attend the biennial convention of the national union, and attendance of officers or other union representatives at other conventions, conferences, and smaller meetings are extremely important to both formal and informal intra-union communications.

Obviously, the effectiveness of meetings as a means of communication depends on attendance and the ability and willingness of those who attend to carry information back to other union members. Many members, and in this the members of Local 630 are not unique, simply do not have enough interest to participate in the union's routine affairs. This lack of regular participation in the union meetings inevitably results in a weakness in the union's chain of communications.

A question concerning attendance at union meetings brought replies showing that, although about 70 per cent of the workers attended union meetings at some time, the number who had attended the last three meetings before the study was made was considerably less.

TABLE 11. Attendance at Last Three Union Meetings

Number of last three meetings attended	*Per cent responding*
None	38
One	26
Two	16
Three	9
No response	11

Of eight questions in the poll that sought to test the extent of the worker's knowledge of union affairs, response from those who said they had attended all of the last three meetings showed, in each instance, that such workers were considerably better informed than those who had not attended. Workers who had regularly attended union meetings were, for example, better informed about the organization of the Joint Board. More of them indicated that the union had made its main objectives (besides obtaining wage increases) clear to them, and more were acquainted with the terms of the labor contract. In all of these responses, the difference in the degree of understanding of the participating and non-participating members was significant, ranging from 26 to 32 per cent better for participating members. While it is possible that those attending union meetings were already most interested in union affairs and had profited from all sources of information more than the average member, the responses suggest at the least that participation in meetings helps to make the information "stick."

Response to another question further illustrates both the importance of attendance at meetings to intra-union communications and also the apparent lack of success of other media in supplementing the union meeting. The union used various channels to distribute information concerning its expenditures. Financial statements were issued periodically in pamphlets and also in the local's newspaper, both of which were available in the union hall and also distributed by shop stewards. Financial reports were made in union meetings. Nevertheless, almost half of the respondents said that they did not receive any accounting of their union's expenditures. The response of those members who had been in regular attendance at union meetings as compared with the response from those whose attendance had been irregular is strikingly different as is shown in the following table.

TABLE 12. INFORMATION ABOUT UNION EXPENDITURES

Receive information about union expenditures	Response according to last three meetings attended				Per cent of total responding
	None	One	Two	Three	
	Per cent responding				
Yes	19	33	48	68	32
No	62	47	39	19	49
Not sure	16	14	9	3	12
No response	3	6	4	10	7

2. Publications

For the benefit of the membership in all eight of its affiliated locals, the Central Jersey Joint Board of the Textile Workers Union publishes a bi-monthly paper, entitled the *Central Jersey Textile News*. This is edited by the Joint Board's educational director, and is distributed to Johnson & Johnson employees by the departmental shop stewards. By no means as elaborate as the company's *J & J Bulletin*, the Joint Board's publication devotes much more space to reporting current news of labor-management activities, and the personal news items, while numerous, apply to a broader area than the membership in the Johnson & Johnson plants. Although some photographs and cartoons are published in each issue of the *Central Jersey Textile News*, these do not have the professional quality of the photographs reproduced in the company's magazine.

In addition to the Joint Board's *Central Jersey Textile News*, members of Local 630 receive a national union newspaper, *Textile Labor*, issued twice a month. This paper is printed in the conventional newspaper style and is mailed to the workers' homes, bringing news of the national labor scene as well as a number of feature articles and editorials. A woman's page is included, and national union policies and programs, such as political action, are featured. Many additional pamphlets and publications of the Textile Workers are available to members of Local 630 on request or distributed by departmental stewards.

A comparison of employee attitudes toward union and management publications provides some clue to their relative effectiveness. As indicated in Table 2,[1] 91 per cent of the workers said that they sometimes read the company magazine and 83 per cent of the workers read nearly every issue. The union periodicals were found to be not nearly as popular. The workers' response regarding the extent to which they read union periodicals and pamphlets is tabulated below.

TABLE 13. EXTENT TO WHICH UNION LITERATURE IS READ

Periodicals	Per cent responding	
	Sometimes read	Read nearly every issue
Central Jersey Textile News	52	26
Textile Labor	25	10
Pamphlets	Have read at least once	Has been most useful
TWUA—How it Works	18	8
Union constitution	36	15
Labor agreement	39	18

Workers may have preferred the *J & J Bulletin* to the parallel publication of the union's Joint Board for several reasons. The company is willing and able to spend more money on its publication, and hence is

[1] See p. 36.

able to present a more professional job. Also, the *J & J Bulletin* has been published for a much longer time than has the *Central Jersey Textile News*. Reading the *Bulletin* may have become a habit. Moreover, the company publication devotes much more space to personal items concerning its New Brunswick employees than the union is able to do in its publication which covers all eight of the locals affiliated with the Joint Board. The union's local publication and national newspaper deal much more frequently with broad issues than does the company magazine. Evidence from other questions in the poll indicates that, whether the information is offered by management or the union, the workers are primarily interested in items that are directly related to their personal lives in the shop or in the home.

The labor agreement, which is of course a document of both union and management, includes one unique feature. Following the formal agreement is an appended section, entitled "Here's How," explaining in simple language each of the provisions of the official agreement. To what extent the "Here's How" section has been successful in gaining wider understanding of the provisions of the agreement was not indicated by the poll. However, the response showed that less than 40 per cent of the literate workers had read the agreement. This is a higher percentage of readers than for the union's constitution, but slightly less than the percentage that had read the employee handbook and the group insurance booklet.[1] It is apparent from another response that more workers depended on the shop stewards for an explanation of the agreement than read it themselves.[2]

3. *Workers' Education*

The Textile Workers Union places considerable emphasis on workers' education. Believing in the democratic administration of their union, the leaders feel that workers' education is essential not only to the democratic operation of a union but also to the maintenance of a democratic society in general. To help local organizations in their training and educational programs, the national office of the union maintains an educational department and traveling representatives whose services and publications are readily available to the "grass-roots" membership.

Although perhaps not as much opportunity for training is offered to Johnson & Johnson employees through their local union as is provided by the company's personnel department, the union and its Joint Board also have an ambitious training schedule. The core of the union's train-

[1] See Table 2, p. 36.
[2] See Table 15, p. 55.

ing program is a six-week course for shop stewards. Stewards' training is conducted by the Joint Board's educational director, and the course is given annually after the election of new shop stewards. The help received in these courses from nearby Rutgers University has, in the opinion of the educational director, greatly enhanced the value and popularity of this training.

Other courses, such as one on "counseling union members" and another, in sewing, are offered by the Joint Board from time to time. In addition, the local has sent many of its members to various workers' education institutes that are conducted by the national union, the C.I.O., and various educational institutions. The value of representation at these meetings as well as participation in the formal training courses offered by the local is felt to be as much or more in the informal channels of communication they afford and in the building up of a wider interest in the union than in the direct information they may disseminate. The importance of one or another activity in influencing such attitudes is hard to measure, and no attempt to do so was made in this study.

4. *Shop stewards*

The unanimous opinion of the union leaders that the most important part of communications was at the shop steward-worker level was substantiated by the employee response, reported in the previous chapter, showing the dependence of the employees of Johnson & Johnson on the shop steward for explanation of changes in working conditions. Responses to certain other questions in the poll revealed additional employee ideas as to the functions of the shop steward. These made it clear, for instance, that the employees expected to get most of their information concerning the labor contract from the steward and, from past experience, considered him the most helpful source of such information. In contrast, however, it appeared that the stewards had not been effective in getting union ideas unrelated to the work situation to the membership.

The response to a question in regard to the Taft-Hartley bill is an example of the stewards' weakness in disseminating information on broad union aims. The general publicity campaign that was conducted against this bill by the major labor federations and their affiliated organizations is well known. The campaign against the Taft-Hartley bill was also carried on at the local level in New Brunswick. Workers were asked the following question: "Would you say that your union was officially for or against the Taft-Hartley Labor Bill, or didn't the union take a stand one way or another regarding this Bill?" Less than half of the respondents said that the union was against the bill. The remainder indicated either that they did not know what the union's position was with respect to the Taft-Hartley bill, or they made no response. Seven workers said that the union favored the bill. The informational sources (Table 14) mentioned by those workers who knew the union's policy on this matter indicate the relative unimportance of shop stewards in communicating this information.

TABLE 14. INFORMATION CONCERNING TAFT-HARTLEY BILL

Sources of information	Per cent responding
Public newspapers and radio	31
Union meeting	17
Signed petition against the bill	11
Shop steward	9
Fellow workers	6
Other sources	15
No response	11

Cross-tabulation of the response to the question concerning attendance at union meetings and the Taft-Hartley question reveals that 68 per cent of the workers who had attended all three meetings were correctly informed, while only 46 per cent of those who had not attended any of the three meetings knew the union's position. In considering the apparent ineffectiveness of the shop steward in communicating the union's attitude on this public question, the fact must not be overlooked that it was a minor part of the stewards' daily contacts with employees and that the subject was given repeated attention by newspapers and the radio.

The much greater effectiveness of the stewards in explaining the terms of the labor agreement was shown through the response to two questions. The first question permitted a choice of several sources where contract interpretation might have been obtained. More than half of the workers replied that they would ask one of their union representatives. About 20 per cent of the workers replied that they would ask one of their supervisors, and approximately 10 per cent replied that they would ask either their union representatives or their supervisors. Only six per cent of the workers said that they would refer to the contract.

The respondents also were asked: "Which, if any, of the above [sources of information] have been most helpful in explaining the agreement?" The 58 per cent of the workers who gave a definite answer, indicated that the sources which are shown in Table 15 had been most helpful in this respect.

TABLE 15. SOURCE OF EXPLANATION OF LABOR AGREEMENT

Mentioned as most helpful	Per cent responding
Shop stewards	62
Supervisors	14
Shop stewards and supervisors	6
Fellow workers and others	14
No one	4

C. EFFECTIVENESS OF UNION COMMUNICATIONS

1. *Weaknesses*

Three questions that were used in the poll of the 359 production workers at Johnson & Johnson reflect either the failure of the union's communications to reach the membership or the indifference of the members to the information. Less than a third of the respondents were sure that the union distributed information about its expenditures, in spite of the extensive efforts of the union in this regard. About the same number of workers indicated that they had not heard of the Joint Board, although several pamphlets explaining its functions were available and a chart depicting the relation between the Joint Board, the local union, and the national union hung in the union office. Of those who had heard of the Joint Board, only eight per cent could say how the business manager of the Joint Board was selected. Although 68 per cent of those polled felt that the union had made its main objectives clear to them, almost half of these could think of no other reason for joining the union than trying "to get better wages."

2. *Suggestions for improvement*

As in the question concerning management's system of communications, the respondents were given an opportunity to choose among eight suggestions for keeping them better informed about union activities. Of the 87 per cent of the workers responding, most of them checked more than one of the eight suggestions. (See Table 16.)

This response indicates that, most of all, union members expect their shop stewards to bear the brunt of keeping them informed. A close second in the employee suggestions is that the union should use the bulletin boards to better advantage. Apparently, a substantial percentage of the rank and file also desires more information about the progress of negotiations and the outcome of other meetings with management. The number suggesting that union meetings be made more interesting is high in comparison with the number reporting regular attendance at meetings, but interest shown in this response in union or joint union-management

TABLE 16. SUGGESTIONS FOR BETTER UNION COMMUNICATIONS

Suggestion	Per cent responding
Make union meetings more interesting	30
Give more union training courses	9
Post more information on the bulletin boards	46
See that the shop stewards keep in closer touch with their members	53
Have the union participate in the company's training program	10
Have meetings at which the officers of the national union speak	5
Get company officers to speak at union meetings	11
Give out more information about meetings with management	33
No response	13

training courses was low. The implications are that the majority of members prefer to receive information with little effort on their own part.

Only a few voluntary comments were given supplementing the check list. The principal ideas in these were: "Make reading material short and simple"; "Let us know about meetings more than a day or two in advance"; and "Hold union meetings during working hours."

The response of the 34 per cent of the workers replying to the question, "If you could have a talk with the President of your national union, what questions, if any, would you want to ask him?" may be broken down into the following categories:

TABLE 17. SUGGESTED TOPICS OF DISCUSSION WITH THE
PRESIDENT OF THE NATIONAL UNION

Response	Per cent responding
Pertaining to union dues and expenditures	18
Requesting better conditions of employment (wages, hours, job assignment)	23
Requesting more democratic, efficient and fairer union administration	11
Miscellaneous	15
Not sure or no questions	32

The responses to this question had many similarities to the responses to the question regarding a chance to talk with the president of the company. Even more employees failed to respond to this question and more of those who did respond thought they would have no question or didn't know what they would ask. Answers to both questions show a high degree of concern with wages, hours, job assignment, or other particular conditions on which they felt aggrieved.

A considerable number (18 per cent) desired information concerning the determination of dues and how they were spent. Besides providing additional evidence that many members were unaware of the financial reports made by the union to its membership, the critical nature of some of the comments shows how important it is for the union to impress its members with the availability of information even though they do not absorb it. The criticisms of union efficiency and fair dealing were apparently aimed not so much at a lack of information as at the failure of shop stewards to get for the individual worker what, in his opinion, he should have had.

The responses grouped under "Miscellaneous" were related to union policies and to outside conditions. Those related to union policy included such comments as "Go easy on strikes," "Is it true that some locals are for management and not labor?", and "Why unions are not represented in Congress like big business is." Typical comments relating to outside conditions were: "How can the cost of living be reduced?", "How lower production costs in the south are affecting production in the north," and "To help get veterans' housing."

While a minority of the employees polled thus showed some interest in broad union policies or in economic and social problems affecting the welfare of industrial workers, a large majority did not respond and the majority of those who did were concerned with some personal dissatisfaction. This again suggests the existence of a considerable lethargy among the members that must be overcome in developing any informational program beyond subjects of personal interest. Indications of existing broader interests along a minority, however, are not only the few questions on economics which some workers would ask the president of their national union but also the expressed desire of 67 per cent of those polled for more information on decisions of the union's executive board and at least a casual interest of 65 per cent for a company-union sponsored course on wages, prices and profits. Encouraging an expansion of this interest to the point where many more members would actually participate in meetings and educational activities and absorb the information made available to them in print is not one of the least difficult problems of union leadership.

VI. REVIEW OF FINDINGS
OF CASE STUDY ONE

THIS case study reveals both weaknesses and strengths in the company and union informational programs. It also shows the difficulties even in a situation where there are good union-management relations in achieving any but a limited coordination of the union and management programs.

A.   IN REGARD TO MANAGEMENT'S PROGRAM

1. *Recent changes were felt to have made a substantial improvement in the informational program.* Supervisors and employees with five or more years' service agreed overwhelmingly that they now receive more information than when they were first employed. In the supervisors' opinion, the change resulted from (1) the inauguration of regular supervisory conferences, (2) new activities of the personnel department (especially training), and (3) a change in management attitude. The employees believed the change was brought about principally through (1) unionization, (2) improved supervision, and (3) more bulletins and other company publications. The fact that supervisors gave more credit to the training program than did the employees was doubtless influenced by the much larger percentage of supervisors who had participated in training. Since most of the changes mentioned occurred within a few years before the study was made, it is impossible to estimate the relative influence of any one of them. It is clear, however, that as a whole they had made an important contribution to improved communications.

2. *The supervisors (foremen, assistant foremen, and group leaders) were, except on two points, generally content with the information they received, but they tended to underestimate their own importance in the chain of communications.* A substantial number of supervisors expressed a desire for improvement in two respects: (1) that information should be relayed to them in time for them to inform the employees in advance of action; and (2) that more information should be given to them in the course of negotiations with the union.

Higher management, employee, and shop steward responses all showed a higher estimate of the supervisors' contribution to an effective communications system than the supervisors showed for themselves. Responses of the supervisors gave more credit than the employees did to the bulletin board, shop stewards, and rumor. There was apparent need to impress on the supervisors the importance of their explaining to employees posted announcements and information given to the stewards. The supervisor's role in these two respects was emphasized by the fact that employees greatly preferred to get information on matters affecting their jobs directly from him or from the shop steward.

3. *Publications were rated low in comparison with other sources of specific information by both supervisors and employees.* Nevertheless, the employee poll showed a very high reader interest in the employee magazine and a reasonably high interest in reprints of articles by the chairman of the board of directors. This suggests that the value of these publications may lie principally in building up the prestige of the company among the employees and promoting a feeling of being a part of a successful industrial enterprise. The percentage of employees that had read special pamphlets issued by the company indicates that these are used largely as reference handbooks, with principal reliance on supervisors or personnel staff for an explanation of such matters as group insurance. For specific information, verbal communications were preferred to the written word, except as the latter supplemented the former.

4. *The union organization provided an important adjunct to management's channels of communications.* While top management and supervisors recognized the value of the union in facilitating communications, the employees expressed a desire to have even more information given to them through the union officers and shop stewards. Employee response also indicated that the mere fact that they were represented by a union promoted a feeling that information could be obtained more easily from management.

B. In Regard to the Union's Informational Efforts

1. *Union meetings appeared to be the most effective formal means of communication between officers and membership.* According to the employee poll, the workers showed an acquaintance with union policies and activities almost in direct relationship to their attendance at union meetings. Poor attendance was a serious weakness in the union's informational system.

2. *Shop stewards, like the supervisors, were unaware of the importance of their own role in communicating information and ideas to the workers.* Almost twice as many workers suggested that stewards "keep in closer touch with their members" than that the union "make its meetings more interesting." Answers to various other questions indicated that many more employees looked to the steward for information on matters, such as wage determination, than had received such information

from him in the past. This comparatively greater interest in the shop steward as a source of information substantiated other indications of the employees' preference for informal, verbal, on-the-job communication, a preference continually recognized by the union leaders in their discussion of objectives and methods.

3. *Printed material distributed by the union was a relatively ineffective means of communication.* The response of the group polled indicated that only a little more than half of the membership read the *Central Jersey Textile News*, the union's local bi-monthly publication. Responses to other questions revealed that a much smaller proportion of workers had absorbed important information—such as the financial report of the union—that had been published in the paper as well as distributed in leaflet form. The union had definite financial limitations on what it could spend on publications. Thus while it recognized many ways in which its publications could be improved, it could not do a great deal about it if the improvements were to involve large expenditures. For this reason, as well as because of the preference of employees for verbal communications, the union leaned most heavily on personal channels.

The exception to the worker's greater approval of the spoken word was their interest in announcements on bulletin boards. Interpreting as a whole the responses to several questions, a definite impression is gained that employees would like to see joint announcements from management and union on the bulletin boards and, in addition, a further explanation of these announcements from their supervisor and steward.

4. *In general, members were not well informed on union policies, organization, and aims.* Considering the means the union has used to keep its members informed, the general knowledge revealed by the poll was low. This may have been due to the comparative newness of the union. The total results, however, suggested the need for study of all the media of communications for possible improvement.

C. In Regard to the Interaction of the Union and Management Informational Programs

1. *The close connection between union-management relations and communications*

This study demonstrated in many ways that good union-management relations are a helpful background to the most satisfactory development of in-plant communications, and that improved communications in turn tend to improve union-management relations. It was clear that agreement on basic issues had to precede agreement as to facts to be given to the workers and the channels through which the information should be transmitted. Both parties recognized that good intra-company and intra-union communications were important to good union-management relations at the shop level. Foremen and stewards had to understand what their respective officers had agreed on before they could give the same explanation to employees. Agreement at this level, it was felt, was ultimately as important as agreement at the top.

The reverse side of the picture was also recognized. Open conflict or unallayed fears on either side not only would tend to block joint efforts in communications but would seriously undermine employee confidence in the reliability of the information or explanation given them.

2. Employee desire for joint union-management communications

The employee poll showed that while the workers believed that unionization had been the most potent influence towards improved communications, they were conscious of being members of both the union and the company organization. As the focal point of communications from both sides, the employees wanted information that had the approval of both parties. Given a choice, the workers preferred meetings at which superintendents *and* union officers would explain new policies rather than for meetings with the superintendent alone; preferred company officers rather than national union officers speaking at union meetings; preferred joint instruction on wages, prices, and profits rather than a course given unilaterally by either management or the union. On a number of subjects, the employees liked to be able to secure accurate information from either the foreman or the steward. Joint communications or having the same information available from either of the organizations of which they as workers were members seemed outstandingly desirable to the rank and file.

3. Common union-management goals and problems

In their common aims seeking to develop better informed and thus more effective employees, union members, and citizens, the union and management faced certain common problems. One problem of considerable concern to both was the need of impressing foremen and stewards with the importance of their roles in keeping the employees informed. While training was being given to these first-line representatives, there was apparent need for more, especially for the stewards. The timing and completeness of information given to supervisors and stewards were also important factors in their effectiveness in communications. Both groups felt that they were sometimes by-passed and resented this.

Another problem that both union and management commented on and that was substantiated in the employee poll was the lack of worker interest in subjects outside the job situation. Representatives of the company and the union agreed that the objectives of their informational program included arousing greater interest among the workers in self improvement and in broad social and economic questions. Careful appraisal of the reasons for this apathy would seem to be essential to sound future planning in regard to the scope and media of communications and the extent of joint efforts.

4. Limitations to the coordination of management and union informational programs

While employees showed a high interest in joint communications, both management and union representatives pointed out definite limitations to such joint action. In practice, announcements on agreements reached between union and management were made almost simultaneously through the two organizational channels, but most printed media, other than the contract and the supplementary explanation, were issued separately. The idea of joint issuance of periodicals or pamphlets was considered impractical primarily because of the extensive, time-consuming discussion such a course would require. The union's attitude also was that, on certain subjects, it did not want to challenge management's statements but neither did it wish to put its stamp of approval on them. In other cases, it was felt that an attempt at a joint statement might bring to the fore issues that both sides were willing to minimize for the sake of continuing friendly relations.

In spite of these apparent limitations, management in particular felt there was room for greater joint action. An effort was being made towards cooperation between management and the union in planning and presenting the training offered the employees. The initial success in this development suggested the practicability of further mutual support of training dealing with non-controversial matters. The attitude of both sides, however, revealed a recognition of the need always to consider the effects of communications on union-management relations as well as on management-employee or union-member relations. The employee poll indicated that workers have considerable loyalty to both the company and the union. The attempt of either management or union to use an informational program to arouse greater worker interest would seem to stand best chance of success when it is based on full acceptance of this dual loyalty.

CASE STUDY TWO:

ESSO STANDARD OIL COMPANY
(BAYWAY REFINERY)
AND THE
INDEPENDENT PETROLEUM WORKERS

VII. BACKGROUND OF THE CASE

THE individual refinery in which this study of communications centered is part of a vast organization through which petroleum and its by-products are produced, refined, manufactured, transported, and sold. The Bayway Refinery of the Esso Standard Oil Company, an important part of this process, is largely self-contained with its own management responsible for its effective functioning.

Communications within the refinery are an indivisible part of its operation, and the content of communications is principally the day-to-day flow of information and ideas related to operations. Communications are, however, also affected by the refinery's relationship to other divisions of the larger corporate organization. Consequently any helpful description of the background of communications in the one refinery must include salient facts concerning the relationship with the higher management levels of Esso Standard and with the parent company, as well as facts concerning the intra-refinery organization.

A. THE BAYWAY REFINERY

The refinery located in Linden, New Jersey, has been described by the company as "one of the world's great petroleum refineries." Its operation was begun with the firing of the first battery of stills in January, 1909. By 1948, the number of employees had expanded to 4400, its operations were scattered over some 1600 acres, and it was processing as high as 175,000 barrels of crude petroleum a day. Its principal equipment includes three atmospheric pipe stills, a vacuum pipe still (under construction), ten thermal cracking coils, a catalytic cracking unit (with an additional larger "cat" cracking unit under construction), a large chemical products plant, and tank fields with storage capacity of 13,-000,000 barrels.

The work of this huge plant is carried on mainly by a process division, responsible for the actual operation of the units, and the mechanical division, responsible for their maintenance and, to a limited extent, new construction. Both divisions head up to the superintendent of the refinery, who is assisted by various coordinating staffs. Two separate departments—operation analysis and the laboratories—provide technical advice. Within the two main divisions, the responsibility for carrying on operations and maintenance falls ultimately on the foremen. These first-line members of management must combine technical know-how with a sense of the interrelationships involved. More than that, they must be able to turn impersonal policies into concrete practices, and in doing so gain the understanding and cooperation of the employees working with them.

B.   RELATIONSHIPS WITH HIGHER MANAGEMENT LEVELS

Vertically the overall organization of which the Bayway refinery is an integral part extends from the refinery employee to the board of directors of the Standard Oil Company (New Jersey). The principal levels of management in between the superintendent of the refinery and the board of the parent company are the New Jersey Works, the East Coast Manufacturing Division, the Manufacturing Division of Esso Standard Oil Company, and the directors of Esso Standard.

The stated organizational policy of the parent company is that "Each company affiliated with Standard Oil Company (New Jersey) manages and controls its affairs through its own directors and officers." The parent company operates in an advisory capacity to the managements of the affiliates, and policies emanating from the head office are in the form of suggestions that may or may not be followed by the operating managements. The parent determines the general long-run objectives; subsidiaries are given great leeway in developing their own policies and plans to carry out their responsibility in gaining these objectives.

In the owner-management relationship between parent and subsidiary, the communication bonds are close. Coordinating committees and an extensive system of meetings facilitate frequent personal contacts between parent and affiliate personnel and between representatives of the same levels of different subsidiaries. A wide range of printed pamphlets and periodicals issued by the parent go to members of all the operating managements and in some cases to the employees of all subsidiaries.

Present communications in any situation are clearly affected not only by the policies as of the moment but also by their historical development. In Esso Standard, the historical influence of the parent company is notable in the encouragement of the use of "pooled judgment" throughout the entire organization and in the assistance given in the development of high standards of personnel practice.

Jersey Standard has pioneered in progressive personnel policies for 30 years. Following the Bayonne strikes of 1916-1918, Clarence J. Hicks, who had just helped establish a plan of employee representation in the Colorado Fuel and Iron Company was made executive assistant to the president of Standard Oil Company (New Jersey) to aid in the development of sound employee relations. This move set in motion forces that not only resulted in employee representation units in the various subsidiaries, but also in formal personnel departments and personnel policies of uniformly high standards. Many of these basic policies are still in effect in the Bayway refinery although modifications and liberalizations have been made over the years.

Because of its size and location, Esso Standard may have been influenced by the parent to a greater degree than other subsidiaries. Accounting for a large proportion of the domestic sales and with central offices in New York, Esso serves both as one of the testing grounds for new programs and as an important source of personnel for positions in the parent company.

As in the case of the parent, the Esso directors are full-time officers, and with few exceptions are career employees, combining an immediate knowledge of specific problems with an overall understanding of the general direction of the company. They are assisted by various staffs charged with correlating the administration of policies in the individual refineries. While the staff is clearly distinguished from the line, the more important staff functions parallel the line down to the refinery level. The coordinators and other special staffs are a significant part of the communications system in Esso both in respect to operations and personnel.

To facilitate both upward and downward communications in the development and application of policies, the directors of Esso Standard have worked out an extensive system of meetings. Some of these—such as the manufacturing meeting where the managements of the refineries meet with the manager of the East Coast units—deal principally with broad operating policy. They are designed to keep upper management informed on operating problems and to bring the refinery managements into contact with thinking at the top level.

About the basic line of communications between the manufacturing manager and his general superintendents revolve many supplementary lines designed to handle particular problems. These involve more specialized meetings. Top management likes to think that no policy is adopted without full discussion and is willing to risk overdoing meetings to this end. Some of these meetings are called in connection with special problems of particular products or operations, others relate to more general operating techniques. Technical meetings held for operating personnel help to bring the broad problems of the company closer to the refinery management. Typical of these meetings are the mechanical superintendents' conferences, the process superintendents' conference, and the more frequent chemical products conferences.

The management of Esso Standard clearly recognizes that personnel matters cannot be separated from operations. In the general manufacturing and technical meetings, personnel policy may be discussed incidentally or as an important part of a manufacturing or technical development. Special meetings may deal principally with one or more personnel problems. The point of view of the employee-relations staffs from the Esso head office and the refineries is given special consideration at the semi-annual general superintendents' meeting where a full day is devoted to employee relations.

Personnel policies are handled by line officers as a major part of their work. This is true at the foreman's level as much as at the president's. The employee relations department, like the manufacturing coordinators, is set up to inform, advise, and coordinate, but the line at all levels is expected to understand and effectuate personnel policy. Details of policy are, however, continually supplied by the employee relations staff to the line. To help them fulfill their informational and coordinating functions, personnel managers of the different operating units get together periodically. Personnel policy is the frequent subject of both up and down and horizontal exchange of information, due in part to the common nature of personnel problems throughout all units of the corporation, and in part to the fact that certain specific personnel policies (notably benefit plans) are established on a corporation-wide basis.

A great variety of printed material as well as person-to-person contacts supplement the system of meetings. A monthly newsletter, containing a résumé of the principal events in each refinery and summaries of what top management is doing, goes to all the key people in the organization. The management bulletin, distributed to all supervisors, is more general and less comprehensive but it too contains pertinent information on company policies. Such publications as *Your Job*, the benefit plan booklets, and material on the training program, are available to executives, supervisors, and employees. In addition, reprints of speeches, several company newspapers and magazines, correspondence and the like serve the purpose of bringing the activity of top management to the attention of people at the refinery level.

The impression gained from the study of the means of exchanging information and ideas between the refinery and higher levels of Esso Standard, and between Esso Standard and the parent corporation, is that of continuous and close communications.

C.   THE UNION AT BAYWAY

The employees at the Bayway refinery have had organizational representation since the industrial representation plan was adopted there in 1918. When the Wagner Act made it necessary to dissolve this plan, the employees formed an independent association which was disestablished by order of the National Labor Relations Board in 1942. At that time the International Oil Workers (CIO) sought to organize the Bayway refinery, and a Labor Board election was held. The Independent Petroleum Workers of New Jersey won by a vote of four to one, and were certified as the bargaining agency for all wage and salaried employees (excluding only supervisory, technical, and confidential personnel).

Through collective bargaining, the Independent Petroleum Workers participate in developing the personnel policies that govern wages, hours, and working conditions of the employees in the refinery. Union officers and committees meet frequently with management and these meetings are important in the development and administration of policy. Thus the union provides the machinery for channeling and presenting the workers' interests to management.

The first-line representatives of the union are the stewards who are elected in the ratio of approximately one steward to every forty men. They carry on the day-to-day union-employee business in the shop. Immediately above the stewards are the union representatives of the 44 departments or trades. These 44 representatives along with the officers make up the executive board of the union. The union bargaining machinery consists of committees covering four main areas: overall wages, hours, and working conditions; individual job rates; grievances; and seniority. Parallel committees represent wage employees and salaried employees.

These committees and the union organization as a whole fit closely into the refinery organization. The union's functions are recognized by management and play an important part in the personnel side of operations. These functions are limited almost exclusively to matters directly concerned with the workers of the Bayway refinery, although the Independent is represented on the coalition committee whose membership is made up of the manufacturing unions in the company.

VIII. COMMUNICATION OBJECTIVES

IN determining what information is important in a company, how it should be disseminated, and what results are expected from it, all the factors which mold the character of the company as an institution play a part. Extensive interviews with refinery executives, union officers, and upper management executives revealed different attitudes towards communications depending on the individual's particular interest. However, taken as a whole, their composite ideas show a fairly clear picture of a common understanding of the broad purposes of the company.

A. MANAGEMENT'S VIEW

The comments of executives in response to a question as to what they considered to be the principal aims in maintaining effective communications throughout the organization included both general aims and ideas as to how the aims might be attained. The chief points brought out are outlined below.

1. *The development of attitudes*

The necessity of good communications in the development of desired attitudes was stressed by all levels of management. In refinery management, this was expressed principally in terms of understanding among supervisors and employees; among the higher executives, this included the broader point of view of gaining reasonable uniformity of attitudes throughout all levels of the organization. Gaining a wide understanding and common attitudes in two subject areas were mentioned in particular.

a. Corporate responsibility

The foreword to Standard's labor policy published in 1918 explains that Standard operates "on the fundamental proposition of a square deal for all concerned: the employees, the stockholders, the consumers of the company products, and the general public." In general the feeling is that this has become a reality, and that executives have come to think in terms of the whole organization rather than a particular interest. If this ideal of corporate responsibility is to be kept a reality, however, it is necessary to indoctrinate the on-coming executive. Training programs, continually available written statements of policy, and absorption by observation and personal contact are all important aids in this respect.

b. Employee relations philosophy

The philosophy governing employee relations throughout Jersey Standard's organization has been repeated at every opportunity since it was adopted in 1918. In broad terms, it encompasses fair wages and fair dealing, individual opportunity, group representation, and employee security. A number of the executives interviewed, especially in the refinery, felt that the organization was so well permeated with this philosophy that it was of minor importance in daily communications. Some of the higher executives, however, considered it a matter always to be kept in the foreground. Evidence of their thinking was the place given to employee relations in planning executive and supervisory training, in the attention given to employee relations problems in general management meetings, and in the many publications stating the principal points of the employee relations philosophy.

The comments of executives in the refinery reflected to a large extent the ideas of upper management in what was sought through communications. This similarity of thinking in itself suggested the success of the efforts of top management to develop a uniform acceptance of the philosophy of corporate responsibility and sound employee relations. The comments also showed, however, different interests in communications depending upon the individual executive's immediate responsibilities.

The refinery executives were inclined to feel that favorable employee attitudes were gained more by doing than by telling. The most important content of communications, from their point of view, was information necessary to get the job done. This, it was emphasized by several, included both up and down communications with the chance of lower levels to comment on proposed action and an explanation from above as to why one course of action rather than another was followed.

One executive, who stressed the principal need of keeping foremen informed and holding them responsible for transmitting essential information, felt that the foreman's "attitudes and way of treating people" were also very important in gaining employee understanding. A department head commented that "it is important to concentrate on particular information and to build attitudes on the basis of action rather than orders. Actually, important matters of policy are apparent in the application of benefit plans, employment policies, and the like. It is from these *actions* that people in the company form their attitudes."

This common opinion among Esso executives that "actions speak louder than words" tended to discount the public relations aspects of communications. Nevertheless a few of those interviewed recognized the impact of non-company sources of news upon employees and the prestige value of good public relations to all members of the organization. Company practice also suggested a greater recognition of the interrelationships of public and personnel relations than existed among the executives interviewed.

The comments of the refinery executives, who, in general, seemed less concerned than upper management with the development of right attitudes, indicate that long-established company attitudes are taken for granted. The amount of thought given to attitudes by higher executives and staff suggests, however, that the operating executives can take certain attitudes for granted because upper management has long been successful in making its employee relations philosophy a part of general operations.

2. Strengthening the principle of managerial responsibility

Underlying the comments of most of the executives interviewed was a direct or indirect acknowledgment of the company's basic faith in the principle of managerial responsibility. Top management recognizes that, with its operations scattered over so wide an area, it is difficult to build a system of direct communications that will guarantee uniformity of policy. To overcome this handicap of size, a well defined policy of managerial responsibility has been developed. Both the aims and methods of communications are affected by this principle, just as the effectuation of the principle is dependent upon good communications.

The general import of the principle of managerial responsibility is to give individual executives and supervisors a maximum of independence based on their thorough understanding of company policies and objectives. The general policy of promotion from within and such specific training programs as executive development, basics of supervision, and principles of supervision give substance to the principle.

Besides training supervisors and executives in overall company policies and activities as they move upward, top management considers it essential to keep the line executives informed on all aspects of the company's business and to get their ideas and suggestions before making decisions affecting operations for which they are responsible. Management bulletins, regular meetings, and person-to-person contacts all are important in this type of intra-management communications. In regard to organizational responsibility as well as to attitudes, many members of management expressed their belief that the observation of policies in practice was the best means of achieving understanding.

As stated by one refinery executive, "The test of communications is in the active flow of information about particular operations and in an understanding of their importance." In the opinion of another, "communications are the life-line of the company and should be directed primarily towards effective operation." A third, who felt that the "principal aim of communications should be directed at the foremen," was convinced that it was just as or more important for them to understand clearly their own job duties than to "know all about the company and its broad policies."

3. *The development of an informed working force*

Perhaps the most frequently expressed objective of communications was to keep executives, supervisors, and the rank and file fully and accurately informed on matters of importance to the company and to themselves. Typical statements were: "We want our people to know everything about the company that they can absorb." "We want our employees to know how the company does business, and we want them to realize what they are getting in the way of high living standards, good opportunities, and participation in the organization." One executive expressed the opinion that an important aim of keeping everyone well informed was the prevention of false rumors.

The development of an informed working force, it was implied by most of those interviewed, was not an end in itself but a means of insuring desirable attitudes or satisfactory production. Members of the top management of the refinery thus felt that a close acquaintance with higher management thinking and planning was important to their own effective functioning. They felt equally strongly that it was necessary to let employees know "why jobs had to be done as they were expected to be done," if efficiency was to be maintained or improved.

This general aim of an informed working force is reflected in the wide range of company publications, in the indoctrination course and other training programs, and in the emphasis given to meetings and other personal contacts. It is also given increased substance by the extensive use of the principal non-management channel of communications with the employees, that is, the independent union.

B. THE ROLE OF THE UNION

The communications objectives of the Independent Petroleum Workers center about the organization's general objectives and the means of accomplishing them. Primarily the union seeks to make the employees' point of view felt in management councils, to improve the status of the employees as a whole, and to see that individual grievances are settled fairly and promptly. All of these aims of the union require a steady upward flow of opinions, ideas, and facts.

In the opinion of union officers, it is impossible to separate communi-

cations and collective bargaining procedures. One important feature of
the collective bargaining relationship, the open-end contract permitting
the union or management to call for meetings at any time, has, in particular, resulted in almost continuous communication between the two
parties. Both sides agree that bargaining is conducted with a strong factual basis. The union usually goes to a bargaining session with a case
prepared by an investigating committee. The case includes not only a
presentation of employee attitudes and desires but also facts of related
practices in other companies.

The upward flow of information by way of grievance procedure is
similar to that in collective bargaining, except that the principal exchange
of information between management and union may be at the shop level
—if the grievance can be settled there. The union officers approve of the
settlement of grievances at as low a level as possible. They pointed out,
however, that the satisfactory handling of grievances required that foremen and stewards be very well informed on contractual matters.

Keeping their stewards and representatives informed so that they can
handle their union responsibilities and keep the employees in turn well
informed is the principal objective of downward communications. The
union officers feel strongly that informing the employees is the union's
province and responsibility. This includes information on all matters of
interest to employees, whether within the area of bargaining or not. The
whole machinery of representatives and stewards operates to serve and
inform the members. Comparatively little dependence for union communications is put on the written word.

The indivisibility of the upward and downward flow of communications is illustrated by the way employees are kept informed on negotiations. The officers do not consider it necessary to keep employees
posted on negotiations unless there is a stalemate. However when wages
are being bargained over and there is possible need for a referendum, it
is considered essential to keep employees regularly up to date so they
may understand fully the issues involved before being asked to vote
on them.

The union, concerned only with bargaining for the employees of the
Bayway refinery, has no interest in using its informational efforts to
sway the employees on political issues or community activities. Participation in the coalition movement of the various independents is considered by the Bayway union to be primarily informational. Representation
on the coalition committee fits into the union objectives of the upward
and downward flow within the refinery since the Bayway union seeks,
through the interchange of information with the other independents, to

be better prepared to present a good case for the point of view of its own members.

The general impression gained from interviews with management representatives and union officers was that there were many points of common interest between management and union objectives in communications. The main elements of management's program had been accepted by the union. Its leaders expressed no great suspicion of management's motives nor distrust of the information. They were inclined to look upon some of the printed material issued by the company as neither very important nor very effective, but they showed no resentment against the quantity, nor fear that it would detract from the status of the union. The leaders were interested in communications within the upper levels of management insofar as they dealt with personnel and labor policies. They were almost as interested as management in having well informed supervisors.

This generally favorable attitude of the union toward management's communications was doubtless influenced by management's recognition of the function of the union in refinery communications. Management representatives reported repeatedly and consistently that they went far beyond the requirements of collective bargaining in consulting with and informing the union officers and representatives.

But in spite of the wide agreement in objectives, the management and union informational aims were by no means identical. The union, for example, often gave the employees an interpretation quite different from management's on such matters as the company's profit policy and the application of benefit plans. Insofar as management and employee interests differ, the union aims to fulfill its responsibility in keeping its members aware of the issues involved.

IX. COMMUNICATIONS IN THE UPPER LEVELS OF THE REFINERY

ALL the elements of company organization involved in internal communications are represented in the refinery. While it functions within the general perspective provided by the parent company, it is in many respects a distinct entity. The present study reports on an examination of the refinery's communications problem undertaken to find out (1) how well policy was understood and (2) how well the information system has served the needs of line management and the union. The reactions of individuals were explored at the top refinery level, the foremen-steward level, and the employee level. Throughout, the aim was to look at those communications of most significance to the company as an institution, and to see how they were related to the individual job requirements and performance.

The Bayway refinery is run by the general superintendent, his assistant, and two main division heads. Immediately below them are the department heads and general foremen, and working with them are the several staffs. All in all the "upper levels" consist of some forty individuals who might be called the refinery management. Parallel to this organization are the top union officials: the president, vice president, secretary, treasurer, and the important committee heads, about ten key individuals. Over half of this group of fifty people were interviewed. They were asked what elements of company policy they felt they should know, what information they thought should go to those below them, and what type of information they needed to perform their jobs.

A. THE FUNCTIONS OF COMMUNICATION IN THE REFINERY MANAGEMENT

Generally the members of the refinery management view the daily operations not in terms of the development or administration of policies but in terms of getting the work done. Their chief concern is with how a job is to be accomplished and only to a lesser degree with why it is to be done. Yet the refinery must operate within the general policy framework established by upper levels of Esso Standard and the parent corporation, and it has both an opportunity and a responsibility to help develop the framework. It also has the responsibility of working out, with higher management, adjustments in policies that may be needed for the most effective functioning of the refinery.

Thus communications within the upper levels of the refinery encompass policy development, planning, coordination of various operations, direction of specific areas of operation, and an understanding of the ideas and policies back of the operations. The refinery management is a kind of power substation of communications between the higher levels of the company and the supervisors and employees of the refinery. But it also is the original source of part of the downward flow of information, and is responsible for the establishment and maintenance of the machinery of communications within the refinery. Finally, and of not least importance, it must keep itself informed on what is going on within the plant and on matters outside that directly limit or influence refinery activities.

The determination of the system of communications within the refinery is largely the responsibility of its top executives. However, like many policies, decisions regarding the use of one or another channel of communication are influenced to a large extent by methods worked out and used at higher levels of the company. Likewise methods of communications established by the top management of the refinery and used within its immediate area may be used to varying degrees for intradepartmental exchange of information.

For example, the pattern of primary line responsibility for communications, with staff assistance and supported by a system of meetings, was set by the parent corporation. It is followed by the top management organization of Esso Standard, and carried into the top level of the refinery. But, in general, less emphasis is placed on written material as a medium of communication within the refinery than at higher levels, and the extent to which meetings are used by department heads and supervisors varies considerably between departments.

In agreement with their emphasis on the operational content of communications, the refinery line executives stressed aims and problems of communications related to organization and operation. Staff personnel were more often concerned with difficulties preventing a general and wide understanding of goals, background policies, and facts of the company's progress. Most of the specific problems mentioned by both groups were related to one or another method or channel of communication and are discussed below along with the descriptions of the various channels.

B. RESPONSIBILITY OF THE LINE ORGANIZATION

As reported in the previous chapter, one of the important objectives of communications in the Esso Standard Oil Company is to reinforce the company's basic principle of managerial responsibility. In accord with this principle, the line organization itself is the chief circuit of communications. The informational activities of staff personnel, the whole system of meetings, and written materials all aim to strengthen the understanding of the line executives of their total jobs and their ability to transmit this understanding to others. Even the union, which has its own objective in communications and plays an important role in management-employee communications, is dealt with by the refinery management in such a way that the line responsibility for communications is emphasized and strengthened rather than by-passed.

Communications through the line organization involve not only direct person-to-person exchange of information, which is felt to be essential, but also all the other methods of communication used in the refinery. The two most important points in respect to the line organization's responsibility are (1) that each unit head understands and accepts his individual responsibility for communications and (2) that he knows how to use effectively the supplementary media and channels.

The first point, acceptance by the executive of responsibility for satisfactory communications within his operating unit, is influenced to a large extent by his understanding of his job and its relationship to the organization as a whole. "The real purpose of an information program," the general superintendent stressed, "is to give independence and responsibility to each executive." The idea is that a man should know what is expected of him and be given a chance to learn what he needs to know without having to depend in detail on his immediate superior.

Despite the active support of the refinery management, difficulties were found in making the policy of individual responsibility effective. In the first place, it requires clear lines of authority and these sometimes are obscured in the process of change. Secondly, individuals must be in the habit of thinking for themselves and acquiring information; the military-like rule of the earlier days was believed to work against such habits in some cases. And thirdly, the exact limits of independence must be defined and followed up or the policy becomes ineffective.

Within the refinery, organizational responsibility refers principally to the department heads and general foremen. Broadly speaking there are four different types of situations—maintenance and construction, the straight process units (manufacturing), the chemical products (special manufacturing units), and the technical and other staff groups. The effectiveness of the policy is therefore to be measured by the extent to which inherent difficulties have been overcome in each of these areas.

In the trades, which employ the largest group of workers in the refinery, the lines of authority between the main office and the field are fairly clear-cut; each trade foreman reports to the craft superintendents who in turn report to the mechanical superintendent. The problems reported were felt to stem from the habits which went with a traditional background. The trades have developed a high degree of self-sufficiency. The difficulty is that management would now like to change many of the traditions long followed. In the early days, the boss was there to get the work done; he took his orders and gave them out. It was not for him to make suggestions or cultivate them in his men, nor was he concerned with such things as personnel matters except when they meant authority. Present day management sees things differently. Organizational responsibility means acting independently within broad principles, understanding company policy, and carrying it out without the necessity of constant rechecking.

In the process units, connection with the process superintendent and the general superintendent tends to be closer than is true of the trades. The operation of these units determines whether or not the refinery is meeting its schedule. Thus there is no such natural independence as in the trades. While the line of authority is clear-cut, it is often a more binding line. However, the process department heads are closer in their thinking to the more progressive views of management and in that sense better able to exercise responsibility. Due to the increasingly technical nature of the jobs, younger assistants play an important role, which also furthers general receptivity. But again the ultimate problem is one of defining the area of independence.

Where direct and quick orders are to be transmitted, junior officers lose independence. In more general matters—repairs, personnel, and the like—individual responsibility is asserted. The danger is that even infrequent by-passing tends to restrict the acceptance of individual responsibility. Department heads interviewed complained not that they were by-passed, but that proper follow-up notification was not given. Some also felt that in matters where they should have independence, such as promotions, they were reversed without consultation.

The situations in chemical products and in the laboratories are somewhat different. Isolated to some extent from the principal operations of the refinery, these two smaller divisions have more independence. But problems arise as to exactly what are the connecting links and what are the limits of independence. In particular, inadequacies in the systematic communication of information on matters affecting them and duplication of lines of authority (largely a temporary problem) were felt to be handicaps in the exercise of independent responsibility.

In top management's thinking of organizational responsibility, successful communications are thus measured by the effectiveness of each executive and supervisor in the individual department. The other channels of communications are of varying importance, primarily depending on the extent to which they help the executive to understand his responsibility and supply him with the information he needs.

C. OTHER MANAGEMENT CHANNELS

1. *Meetings*

A rather elaborate system of meetings provides the framework for the regular exchange of information among the management personnel. The general superintendent's weekly meeting on Monday morning is, as one executive phrased it, "the key feature" of the series of regular meetings and of the less formal meetings and conferences held at irregular intervals by the operating and staff departments.

The general superintendent's meeting is an important means of coordinating the activities of all departments. It is attended by the general superintendent, his assistants, the employee relations manager, the head of operations analysis, the coordinator of the laboratories, the process superintendent and one of his coordinators, the mechanical superintendent and his assistant, heads of the major manufacturing units and of the chemical products department, and the head of the accounting staff. The prime purpose is to exchange information on all phases of operations and on problems already met or foreseen.

The procedure in this meeting is to have each man make a report on his unit of operations or staff responsibility, with a chance for questions and comments from other members of the group. In addition, the general superintendent gives out information that all of his department heads should know and comments on developments. Matters for discussion include not only operating plans and problems, but also employee relations, the budget, and any company policy. However, most of the meeting is devoted to subjects directly pertinent to refinery operations rather than to special problems of staff departments.

The information gained by the department heads at the general superintendent's meeting is, in turn, given to general foremen and other principal department executives at departmental meetings held weekly or daily. Examples of these meetings are the process superintendent's Monday noon meeting and the petroleum products meeting held at noon on other weekdays. Attending the former are the heads of all the process departments and representatives from the operations analysis department. The process superintendent reports on information picked up at the general superintendent's meeting and each department head reports on his own problems. The discussion revolves around maintenance, personnel, company policies, schedules for particular orders, quantity, quality, and budget problems. A résumé of topics discussed is sent to each person in attendance and also to the mechanical department.

The noon meetings in petroleum products include the petroleum coordinators, the process superintendent, the heads of the petroleum products departments, and representatives of the operations analysis department. These meetings are most directly concerned with the essential operations of the plant, and their chief function is to coordinate the operating schedules of the various units. Reports are made, problems brought up, and new ideas developed by any member of the group. As in all such meetings, discussion is informal. Although dealing particularly with operating matters, the meetings also may include discussion of the more general problems and policies considered in the general superintendent's or process superintendent's weekly meetings.

A similar hierarchy of meetings is held in the maintenance side of the refinery management, with the regional engineers playing the coordinating role that the petroleum coordinators play in production. The chemical products department has its own regular meetings, as do also employee relations, accounting, and other staff departments. Most of these meetings are weekly, a few daily.

There was general agreement among the executives of the refinery that the whole system of meetings was the core of communications. It provides the opportunity for superintendent and department heads to learn what is going on below and what is on the minds of their subordinates, as well as to pass on to them ideas and attitudes from above. The regular meetings provide the essential background for the more frequent personal discussion. The daily meetings, such as those for the petroleum products departments, may encourage the development of new ideas. However, the special meetings held with staff groups are more likely to go into questions of policy changes and interpretation.

Although most of the executives interviewed expressed the opinion that they were well informed largely through meetings, a number of them had some critical comment. The most frequent criticism was that there were too many meetings taking up too much time. It was hard, however, for anyone to suggest which meetings might be dropped. One suggestion was fewer special meetings and another thought that daily meetings were not always necessary.

Two executives expressed the opinion that meetings were more successful in insuring a good downward flow than a good upflow of information and ideas. It was pointed out that small conferences were more conducive to a free exchange of ideas or to a statement of gripes than a larger general meeting. It was felt, also, that downward communications had a stronger impact, and that criticisms or suggestions of policy often lost their force by the time they got through to the board level where policy decisions are made. The executive making this comment felt that special meetings were more useful in policy development than were the general meetings.

Another weakness in the system of meetings as an important channel of communications is that the regular meetings do not include the lowest level of management. As a result, difficulty was reported in bridging the gap between the general foremen and the line foremen. In some cases, the department head holds meetings of the whole department when there is something of special importance to be explained, rather than depend on the general foremen to spread the word.

These weaknesses pointed out in regard to meetings suggest only that meetings in themselves do not fill the total need for communications. The evidence is that regular meetings provide the most substantial enabling machinery for the effective functioning of the principle of organizational responsibility. Special staff services and conferences, personal contacts, and written media supplement or fill in the details of the general information disseminated through the meetings.

2. Staff

The role of the petroleum coordinator in expediting the work of the process departments and of the regional engineers in the work of maintenance and construction was mentioned in connection with meetings. Communication is the essence of their coordination efforts. Both coordinators and engineers help materially in transmitting ideas upward as well as in gaining understanding of established objectives and of the individual executive's responsibility in attaining them. Their communications are concerned principally with operations rather than with policies. Another staff department, accounting, gives advice on procedures, but also helps in spreading information on cost policies and budgetary matters.

The employee relations staff, dealing with policies and programs applicable to all units of the refinery, has its own special functions in communications. It serves not only as a fact-finding and advisory department to the line organization, but also acts as agent for the general superintendent in being responsible for certain specific activities in connection with collective bargaining, supervisory and employee information, safety, training, employment, transfers, and administration of annuity and benefit plans. These responsibilities are fulfilled both through formal

procedures—meetings, conferences, written announcements, and the like
—and informal relationships. Personal contacts between the employee
relations staff and executives and supervisors were felt to be particularly
important in assuring understanding of personnel matters presented at
the general meetings, and in getting individual executive reaction to the
effect of particular personnel policies in his area of operation.

As stated in Chapter VII[1], greater company-wide uniformity is sought
in regard to personnel policies than for such matters as production and
maintenance. The refinery must follow closely a pattern set at a higher
level. If it feels a policy should be changed, it can and does say so—
through individual contact, meetings, and staff presentation of problems
called to their attention by supervisors. Major changes are made by the
directors for the company as a whole, with the refinery management
being expected to present its problems and ideas. Modifications in policies
to meet special problems within the refinery can be made, and have been
made on the recommendation of the refinery, after thorough consideration by higher levels of management. While the general superintendent,
as the chief executive of the refinery, suggests and recommends such
changes in personnel policy, the basis for his recommendations is
usually developed by the refinery employee relations staff. Members of
this staff carry on much of the consultation with staffs of the East Coast
works and the head office of Esso Standard.

The development and application of management and supervisory
training at the Esso Training Center in Elizabeth (adjacent to the Bayway refinery) demonstrates the close communications between the refinery and the New York office in planning and coordinating activities
that may affect the refinery. The Esso Training Center was established
by the operating company through a training director reporting to the
New York office. The chief function of the center is to work out courses
for all or any part of Esso Standard and to offer the results of its
experience to other subsidiaries of the parent corporation. The Bayway
refinery, which has three members of the employee relations staff assigned to training, works closely with the training staff of the center.

The training program gives much emphasis to management development, and through management courses is felt to be a definite aid to the
improvement of management's effectiveness. Insofar as the courses
provide information on policies and plans, as is true of the basics of
supervision, the training is itself a channel of communications between
top management and supervision. Serving as a supplement to the main
organization channel, the training courses are considered especially help-

[1] See page 66.

ful in reviewing established policy and developing a uniform understanding.

In many other activities, the employee relations staff of the refinery, like the staff of the training center, serves both to aid executives in their informational responsibilities and as a direct channel. The problem is not so much that of making the staff an efficient channel as making sure that the executives use it only as an aid and do not expect it to assume full responsibility for information on personnel matters. The fact that a few executives implied that they did not have to give much attention to personnel information since that was well taken care of by the employee relations staff suggested the need for awareness of this problem. However most of the executives interviewed understood their own responsibility in regard to personnel as well as operating matters.

3. *Written media*

Of the various channels of communications among the refinery management personnel, written media were rated lowest. The *Management News Letter* and *Management Bulletin* were read and counted useful in keeping refinery executives informed on general developments in the company, but not sufficiently pertinent to daily problems to be rated as essential channels.

The distribution of minutes of meetings was considered by a number of men interviewed to be a valuable adjunct to the meetings and the most important form of written material. The minutes provide a permanent record for those who attend, and, when exchanged between departments, make discussion of problems and news of developments accessible to staff and supervisors who do not participate in the meetings. Summaries of certain special conferences, such as collective bargaining sessions, are sent to all executives and supervisors. A number of department heads commented on their usefulness.

Correspondence, like minutes of meetings, is looked upon as a source of information which may encourage better coverage of current problems in the meetings. At least two departments follow the practice of routing correspondence to staff and supervisors, and correspondence with and through the superintendent's office is made available to department heads by means of reading files. Written reports to superiors are a means of upward communications and help bring needed attention to local problems. A number of executives wondered, however, how much of an impression such reports made unless they were the basis for personal or group discussion.

Throughout the interviews with executives, word-of-mouth communication was emphasized more than written matter. The executives were used to talking over developments individually or with the whole top management group of the refinery. Memoranda, minutes, and reports were accepted as helpful supplements to the spoken word. In the opinion of most, written communications could in no way substitute for the personal exchange of information and points of view, but repetition and review in written form were important in strengthening the impact of the oral discussion.

D. COLLECTIVE BARGAINING

Collective bargaining as a form of communications among the upper levels of the refinery has a three-fold aspect. There is the primary exchange of demands and supporting facts in bargaining. Prior to and during negotiations and after an agreement has been reached, the union must keep itself informed on all matters affecting collective bargaining. And, finally, management must keep its own executives and supervisors informed on questions raised, progress in negotiations, agreements reached, and grievances settled.

Communications in bargaining between the refinery management and the Independent Petroleum Workers are influenced greatly by the plan of bargaining, by the attitude towards bargaining, and by the union and management's common understanding as to the role of the union in communications. The open-end contract permits contract changes to be made at any time, and thus encourages frequent discussions between management and the unions. The four dual union committees for wage and salaried employees[1] provide the machinery to handle conferences with management on a systematic basis. Discussion is for the most part, characterized by a full exchange of information and conducted with respect for fact and almost no threat of coercion. Bargaining sessions were described by participants on both sides as "lessons in economics."

The fact that both union and management look upon the union as the chief channel of communications between management and the employees tends to expand the subjects of exchange of information beyond those accepted as within the bargaining area. It also affects the timing and amount of information that top management seeks to give directly to the employees. For example, the benefit plans are, by contract, not subjects for bargaining. Yet in case of changes in benefit plans, the company has first informed its supervisors, then held a meeting for all union representatives, and finally conducted meetings for the employees.

[1] See Chapter VII, p. 69.

Another example of the type of activity on which management keeps the union informed is the use of outside contractors on major construction jobs.

Within the union, the executive committee provides the basic medium for exchange of views and information among the leaders. The committee meets monthly, and this meeting permits the committee as a whole to keep up with the activities of the various special bargaining committees and the findings of the subcommittee doing research. Its members—the 44 departmental representatives—are then expected to inform the stewards on matters with which they should be acquainted and which they should bring to the attention of the employees. A course dealing with interpretation of the contract has been given to the members of the council and shop stewards. In general, the union does not make an effort to keep the stewards and employees up-to-date on negotiations unless there is a stalemate. It does, however, try to get full information to the membership when agreement is reached.

The general superintendent, responsible for bargaining, seeks to keep his executives informed on both developments in negotiation and agreements. Such information is disseminated through the general superintendent's Monday morning meetings, through departmental meetings when the bargaining is particularly applicable to the department, and through memoranda on bargaining sessions issued by the employee relations department. The impression given by the executives interviewed was that they were much interested in the progress of collective bargaining, and accepted the union as something integral to the operations of the plant. They wanted the general foremen to be kept currently informed on union relations and to pass on this information to all their foremen. For the most part, management tries not to influence employees on subjects on which union and management disagree. Foremen are taught to be sources of factual information and to understand fully management's point of view, but not to interfere in areas of management-union disagreement.

The one outstanding matter of union-management communications on which the union ideas differed from management's was the benefit program. Since their provisions are determined at levels above the refinery management, the union, through the coalition committee of manufacturing unions, had sought information from higher management on various aspects of benefits. The union officers at Bayway look upon the coalition committee as an informational rather than a bargaining development—as a means of exchanging information with other independent unions as well as with higher management. The union officers, however, expressed general satisfaction with management's attitudes toward and handling of informational matters. They felt that management adhered closely to its expressed policies of keeping the union informed on all matters that were of direct or indirect interest to it and of using the union as the principal channel of keeping employees informed.

The top executives of the refinery and the union officers thus agree upon the need for keeping their own members informed and of making them responsible for getting information to lower levels. Channels of communications are considered reasonably satisfactory by both sides. While, in common with most unions, the Independent Petroleum Workers seek to expand the area of direct communications, their method of seeking this expansion and management's reaction to its moves are such that communications by both sides continue to be a force for friendly union-management relations.

X. ROLE OF THE SUPERVISORS AND UNION REPRESENTATIVES

T HE shop supervisors are responsible for carrying out the policies that come to them from the refinery management. While lacking any broad authority for decision, they are the crucial links in the company's operational structure. It is their job to translate the broad policies of the company to the work-force and to reflect the attitude of the work-force back to the policymakers. Similarly the union representatives and the stewards are the basic links between the union policymakers and the members.

In the Bayway refinery the average number of employees to each foreman is approximately 15; 75 per cent of the foremen supervise groups of less than 30. The union coverage is somewhat thinner, the average being one steward to every 40 employees. By and large, each employee has both a foreman and a steward whom he sees every day and who knows his particular work problems. The chief exceptions to this on the union side were found in departments somewhat out of the main stream, such as packaging. An experienced union representative kept in touch with such departments.

In an attempt to find out what the stewards and foremen knew of company policy and what they conceived to be their responsibilities in carrying it out, two questionnaires were used: the first was given to 103 of the 349 supervisors picked at random from all departments, and the second to 22 of the 44 union representatives. The union representatives are the top officials for each department forming the union executive board, its governing body. Each one has as many stewards attached to him as called for by the size of his department. Taken together the replies to these two questionnaires revealed both how shop officials react to top policy and what type of information they require in their jobs.

A. Knowledge of Policy

Company policy is important to both supervisors and union representatives. While supervisors are basically administrators concerned with direct orders, much of the employees' impression of what the company stands for is absorbed through contact with them. The union representative is an even more important source of information. As a fellow-worker he has the employees' trust; as an official of the union he has access to what is going on in the company. What he says carries great weight; any inaccuracies in his statements, whether concerned with unilateral or bargained policies, can confuse the situation.

At the shop level as in higher management, immediate manufacturing plans derive from the overall position of the company. However, emphasis in the shop is on local objectives and problems. Personnel relations are likewise handled with due regard for the total company situation. The shop exists as a unit of the company, and the human aspects are greatly affected by the shop's relationship to the larger organization.

1. *Manufacturing policy*

Questions were asked of the foremen and representatives in regard to the affiliates and products of the company, company profits and cost policy, and refinery operations and unit efficiency figures. All of these are subjects that the company has made considerable effort to explain through publications and conferences. Company background is reviewed in a pamphlet issued to all employees and is stressed in orientation and foreman training courses. More current company operations and financial policy are covered in *The Lamp*, a bi-monthly magazine, in the annual report issued to all employees, and in various news articles in the *Esso Refiner*, a bi-weekly company newspaper. The union published a full issue of *Independent News and Views*, the union newspaper, covering their attendance at the stockholders annual meeting and reviewing company profits. Various formal efforts in training courses supplement direct contact with refinery operation.

In general, the responses showed that both foremen and union representatives had a somewhat hazy knowledge of the company organization and its manufacturing policies, but a considerable interest in learning more. In Table 18, the replies to three questions on general policy are compared. The first asked which of five companies, all of them important, were affiliates of Standard Oil (New Jersey). The correct answer called for checking three of the five companies listed. The fact that the supervisors had just recently been exposed to company history in the basics of supervision course gave them an edge, but even so the showing is not impressive. The question on profits, offering a choice of three figures, produced much better results and the interest in profits is noteworthy in the last question in the table. A similar interest is also suggested by the high percentage who answered the question "What subjects would you like to learn more about?" with the statement "company policy" or "profits and business relations."[1] Despite the union's concern with profits, only 12 of the 22 representatives knew the correct figure, although all of this group replying expressed a desire to know more about company finances.

[1] See page 95.

TABLE 18. KNOWLEDGE OF COMPANY AND PROFITS

		Percentage replying	
		Foreman	Union representatives
1.	Affiliates of the company		
	correct	34	9
	wrong	66	91
2.	Profits of company		
	correct	71	60
	too low	11	10
	too high	6	10
	don't know	12	20
3.	Interested in finances		
	want to know more	80	100
	don't want to know more	11	—
	some interest	9	—

Whether the wide desire to know more about the company's financial policy means that the annual report, a rather comprehensive pamphlet with both a general and a detailed description of operations, is unsatisfactory is hard to say. Inevitably a report dealing with such large terms has an aura of remoteness. Profits are a subject about which the union representatives indicate more interest, although less knowledge than the foreman. If the profit message is important to the organization as a whole, it must be correctly understood by the representatives. The company has recently been experimenting with a motion picture on financial operations that may fill the need. At any event, continued effort to simplify and give greater impact to information of this sort appears justified.

Where policy comes more directly home, as in the case of cost control, there is better knowledge of the overall purpose and apparently a considerable interest in the practical details. Much dissatisfaction was voiced, however, about the availability of information. Table 19 shows the results of five questions. The first asked for which of four reasons the program had been adopted, with the choice of two correct and two incorrect answers. This information, which relates to the general conditions of the industry, was available principally in the annual report. In the second question, foremen were asked if their immediate supervisor gave them information on costs, and union representatives were asked if they received such information from any source. The reply of two-thirds that they never receive it or receive it only irregularly would seem to indicate the lack of any consistent flow of cost information at the shop level, a fact already indicated in some of the statements made by department heads and general foremen.

In contrast to this lack of information, is the interest shown in the last three questions reported in Table 19. The third question asked fore-

TABLE 19. INFORMATION ON COST CONTROL AND UNIT EFFICIENCY

		Percentage replying	
		Foremen	Union representatives
1.	Purpose of program		
	Incorrect		
	increase profits by cutting personnel	2	10
	safeguard against contraction	38	30
	Correct		
	improve unit efficiency	83	78
	provide funds for capital expansion	53	41
2.	Availability of information		
	receive information on costs	37	37
	sometimes receive information	27	31.5
	never receive information	36	31.5
3.	Sense of participation		
	have active part or interest	84	100
	no part or don't know	16	—
4.	Opinion as to interest of workers		
	like to hear	45	72
	some like to hear	40	28
	don't like to hear	15	—
5.	Opinion as to amount of information to be given to workers		
	the more the better	95	100
	no help	2	—
	don't know	3	—

men if they felt they had an active part in the cost control program, and union representatives if they were interested in hearing the performance record of their unit or gang. All but 16 per cent of the foremen and all the union representatives answered the question affirmatively with the difference apparently due to the wording of the question. In the fourth question both foremen and stewards were asked if they felt their men were interested in this information, and in the fifth question they were both asked whether the "more information an employee is given about the operations of the company, the more interested he'll be in helping to solve these problems." Each question elicited a strongly affirmative answer. Taken as a group these questions would appear to indicate that interest exists in the cost program at the shop level, but that the present flow of information is inadequate.

The foremen themselves showed considerable interest in learning more about local operations. Asked if they wanted more information about the overall operation of the refinery, 83 per cent answered yes and 14 per cent said somewhat more. In particular, interest was expressed in the integration of the different parts of the refinery, the unit operation, and process operations in general. However, with the foremen, local interest is apparently combined with some concern for such matters as company policy, profits, and business relations. This is less true of the union representatives whose answers to open questions tended to be concerned with more practical job matters rather than either operations or policy.

2. Personnel policy

Standard's personnel program has a history of some thirty years. During this period it has been comparatively well defined and carefully adhered to. Job stability, prevailing wages or higher, liberal benefits, promotion from within, and worker representation are policies that have been reiterated in company publications and speeches. Coming in the wake of a consistent tradition of worker representation, recognition of the independent unions has affected other policies very little. While the Independent Petroleum Workers has set up a completely new organization in the refinery, it has done so with a minimum of conflict.

In Table 20, the replies to three questions on personnel policy are compared. The first asked about established company principles. Five of the seven listed have been actively publicized and practiced by the company. Right answers were picked with varying intensity, the most doubt being shown in the case of career promotions. Actually all five principles have been about equally publicized, but job security, resulting in slow upward movement of personnel, apparently creates doubt as to company policy in regard to promotions.

The second and third questions in Table 20 asked for more specific information about personnel policies. Of those replying, 23 per cent of the foremen and 41 per cent of the union representatives indicated that they did not know which of four plans called for deductions from their pay check. The most common error was in marking one of the company paid plans—survivor benefits—as calling for a pay check deduction. Of more interest is the answer to the third question which asked which of three provisions of the labor agreement were correct. Over 50 per cent of each group erred on this point. Many foremen and union representatives thought the contract provided compulsory arbitration while a substantial number of foremen did not realize that an employee loses all seniority rights after separation of one year from the company.

While the greatest weakness in the general understanding of personnel policy seems to be in regard to the details of the contract, the overall

TABLE 20. KNOWLEDGE OF PERSONNEL POLICY

	Percentage replying	
	Foremen	Union representatives
1. Principles followed		
Correct		
pay prevailing wages	95	64
job stability	88	86
personal security	84	59
full union recognition	77	69
career promotions	57	45
Incorrect		
restrict unions	8	—
hire executives outside	3	—
2. Thrift plan contribution		
correct	77	59
incorrect	23	41
3. Contract provisions		
correct	35	45
incorrect	65	55

understanding of union-management relationships appears reasonably good. Asked which of three statements "reflects your impression of management's attitude toward the union," 78 per cent of the foremen and 50 per cent of the union representatives picked "Treat the union fairly and seek its support in all matters affecting employees even when the union's support is not required under the terms of the labor agreement." Only 12 per cent of the union representatives and 6 per cent of the foremen picked the extreme statement, "Avoid dealings with the union whenever possible."

B. USE AND EFFECTIVENESS OF MEDIA

Throughout the study attention was focused on the media of communications with an eye to observing which were effective for various purposes. Questions of three types were asked: regarding (1) specific publications, (2) success in transmitting information, and (3) overall improvements and suggestions. The diversity of answers indicates the impossibility of prescribing one single medium. Foremen and stewards, it is clear, absorb information from a great variety of sources and favor varied means of dissemination. The important aim would seem to be to consider what information should reach the shop officials, and then to make sure that it is presented through more than one channel.

Two questions were designed to check the readership of publications and pamphlets. Table 21 indicates that readership in almost all cases was high. Foremen could hardly be expected to read the union paper regularly, since it is not readily available to them. The *Management Bulletin*, a monthly publication, covers special issues of company interest. While it suffers at present from news that is not always directly pertinent, its readership is comparatively high.

TABLE 21. EFFECTIVENESS OF PRINTED MEDIA

	Percentage replying					
	Foremen			Union representatives		
	read regularly	read occasionally	don't read	read regularly	read occasionally	don't read
1. Readership of Current Publications						
Esso Refiner	95	5	—	95	—	5
The Lamp	79	18	3	95	—	5
Independent News & Views	13	34	53	81	10	9
bulletin board	70	27	3	86	—	14
Management Bulletin	60	24	16	—	—	—
	read		keep	read		keep
2. Readership of Pamphlets						
safety booklet	95		95	30		70
working rules	85		80	40		55
union contract	85		77	35		65
benefit	83		76	35		60
annual report	74		25	40		40
	verbal		written	verbal		written
3. Media used on particular subjects*						
personnel policies	61		33	76		43
benefit plans	61		76	68		55
contract negotiations	99		19	100		—
rate committee	71		16	100		—
grievances	100		—	100		—

* More than one method was marked in several cases.

In a detailed question analyzing the *Refiner*, it was found that the various sections of the paper are rated fairly evenly. Promotions were given a slight lead by both foremen and union representatives. Editorials and news stories, however, ranked equally with personals, both in readership response and in the written-in suggestions. Clearly the *Refiner* is a dependable means of communicating matters of general significance. The comments made by the union representatives on the *Independent News and Views* stressed an interest in more news of union activities and more frequent publication.

There can be little doubt that publications provide useful media of policy communications. However, on particular subjects, various oral means appear to play an even more important role. Section 3 of Table 21 shows this tendency. Foremen and stewards were first asked how they had learned most about personnel policies, with several alternatives offered. All the oral means took precedence over written media, with basics of supervision and experience topping the list. The next question asked which of eight means were best for disseminating information on benefits. Here opinion was more divided, booklets ranking a little ahead of foremen's or union representatives' explanation. In the last three questions concerning contract negotiations, rate committee activity, and grievances, shop officials specified the media through which they received information. Verbal means were clearly dominant. However, this table can hardly be taken to indicate the superiority of the spoken word in general, since written media are used least in the collective bargaining area. Furthermore, stewards and foremen alike showed in their answers that the means by which information was received were varied and not always reliable. Ninety per cent of the foremen felt that management should put out more information on collective bargaining.

Both foremen and union representatives were asked for comments on the communications system. To the question whether they now received more information than when they started work, approximately two-thirds of each group answered affirmatively. The reasons given for this improvement in each case indicate that general attitudes and conditions within the company are rated higher than specific media. For the foremen, the important factor in improved communications was management policy or attitude (38 per cent), while for the union representatives it was the organization of the new independent union (75 per cent). Foremen conferences and meetings were rated high as also were publications, but both are considered as indications of a change in management attitude. This is borne out in the reasons given by foremen for approving meetings: "more information" and "broader approach," as well as in the desire of representatives for more joint explanation of policy through meetings and training courses. Throughout, the opinion seems to be that information is most valuable where it is backed up by full and frank explanations such as meetings and union conferences tend to promote.

Answers to a general question asking "About what subjects would you like to be better informed?" showed that it is also important for information to be geared to the local situation. Foremen are interested in company policy and business relations but they are equally interested in promotions, training, and refinery operations. The feeling was expressed by one foreman that only through knowing company plans and operations could the individual be made to feel a part of the company. Generally speaking, foremen want to see how their job ties into the company's broad purposes. Quite naturally, union representatives expressed less interest in broad policy than in the immediate aspects of bargaining. Perhaps of some significance is the fact that they expressed a desire to receive information on personnel policy from both the company and the union. Shop officials evidently recognize the importance of information to their jobs and are concerned about what information they get and how they get it.

C. Division of Responsibility

Within the company considerable emphasis is placed on establishing a rather definite view of management and union functions. The top officials of the company consider the lines of authority important; they want them clearly demarcated and adhered to, both as a basis of clear communications and to assure efficient operations. Company objectives are to be achieved through the systematic functioning of each level of management. The union also has achieved for itself a fairly well established place. As the representative of the workers' interest, it participates in policy-making through collective bargaining with the refinery management, and provides a means for its interpretation within the shop.

Table 22 shows the results of several questions on the division of responsibility. Foremen and union representatives were asked: "On which of the following subjects do you think it is your responsibility to give information to your men and on which do you think the foreman (or union representative) should take the lead?" The answers indicate that foremen and union representatives more or less follow the logic that is in the minds of their superiors. Operating instructions, schedule changes, and information on matters connected with the day-to-day conduct of the shop are for the foremen to transmit, although union representatives like to know what's going on. Job descriptions, grievances,

TABLE 22. DIVISION OF RESPONSIBILITY BETWEEN FOREMEN
AND UNION REPRESENTATIVES

Subjects:	Allocation of responsibility					
	percentage of foremen responding			percentage of union representatives responding		
	union rep.	foremen	both	union rep.	foremen	both
Grievances	28	16	56	—	—	—
Operating instruction	1	92	7	18	60	22
Contract negotiations	41	6	53	75	—	25
Training opportunities	—	68	32	18	22	60
Benefits and welfare	—	—	—	33	12	55
Job descriptions	—	—	—	4	13	83

benefits, and training opportunities, all of which involve the individual's status in the shop, fall in an in-between area of concern to both groups. Contract negotiations where the union is representing the workers' interest as it relates to company policy remains generally in the purview of the steward, although more than half the foremen feel they should be well informed in these developments. The most important question at this point is whether the foremen and union representatives receive the information they need to perform their respective jobs.

1. *The foreman*

Section 1 of Table 23 indicates the degree of satisfaction among the foremen with the information they receive on several specific subjects. The only significant deficiency appears in the case of information on the rate committee. While some allowance can be made for the fact that the rate committee has not dealt with all departments, it is nevertheless clear that the day-to-day routine of bargaining is one of the hardest areas on which to maintain an adequate flow of current information.

TABLE 23. THE FOREMEN'S OPINION CONCERNING COMMUNICATIONS

Opinion Regarding	Percentage replying		
	Adequate	In between	Inadequate
1. Adequacy of Information Received on Specific Subjects			
job classification	91	4.5	4.5
rate committee activities	34	27	39
reasons for schedule changes	83	15	2
labor contract	69	26	5
2. Adequacy of Information Given to Workers in Regard to			
job classifications	83	7	10
opportunities to advance	67	10	23
employee interest in reasons for changes in hours or work assignment	95	4	1
3. Relations with Immediate Supervisor	*Yes*	*Sometimes*	*No*
easy to see	93	7	—
willing to talk	88	9	3
available on changes	93	7	—
informed on refinery outlook	47	39	14
4. By-Passing and Unclear Supervision	*Often*	*Sometimes*	*Never*
deal with men directly	13	40	47
more than one boss	26	28	46
consulted on promotion	42	28	30

Replies to a second group of questions (Table 23, section 2) reflect the foremen's opinion as to the adequacy of information given to employees on job classifications and opportunities for advancement and as

to the employee interest in reasons for changes in hours or work assignments. The feeling that employees are not given enough information on
promotions agrees with both the foremen's (Table 20) and the employees' (Table 26) lack of accurate information on this policy.

The degree to which the line foreman succeeds in establishing the
independence of his position is determined largely by his relations with
the general foreman or department head. All current information and
much of a broader nature comes through the direct line of authority;
thus if the foreman is to know where he stands, his relations with his
immediate superior must be good. The next two sets of questions check
this relationship. In reply to the first (section 3 of Table 23), the immediate superior is shown to be generally easy to see, willing to talk, and
available to explain changes. Only in the matter of keeping abreast of
refinery outlook is any dissatisfaction expressed.

A somewhat different story is revealed in the answers to three questions that sought to find out whether foremen felt themselves to be by-
passed or otherwise not sure of their superiors. The questions asked:
"Does your immediate supervisor deal directly with your men on matters of importance such as grievances without consulting you?", "Are
you ever confused by the feeling of having more than one boss?",
"When new supervisors are appointed are you consulted about the
qualifications of your men for these jobs?", about 50 per cent indicated
they were sometimes by-passed. Thus it would appear that although the
general foremen and department heads are easily approached, they
sometimes fail to recognize the interest and prerogatives of their subordinates.

Several other questions sought to establish whether or not the foremen received adequate information to act independently and did so act.
Of the 63 who answered a question on the provisions for training in
their department, 87 per cent felt they could do something and 43 per
cent said they would set up their own program. Eighty per cent felt that
general information on the problems of management and the oil industry was helpful to them in their job, marking management meetings as
the best way of getting this information, with trips to other plants as a
principal or additional means. Sixty per cent felt that management was
interested in their opinions on collective bargaining and that they could
express them through their immediate supervisor. Replies to several
questions, however, revealed considerable dissatisfaction over the information received on bargaining activities. Sixty-two per cent heard of
negotiations after they were completed, and sixty-eight per cent of those
answering would like to have heard before. Rumor was the predominant

means by which foremen found out about the union stand, and over 90 per cent indicated that they would like to know more about the company position.

Foremen's replies indicate on the whole that they are well informed and know what to do on matters pertaining most immediately to their job. This in itself goes a long way to fulfilling management's concept of their responsibility. However, the fact that in several instances they feel by-passed and that they are frequently dissatisfied with the information given them on collective bargaining defeats the full achievement of this objective and leaves areas for improvement.

2. The union representative

The union representative's position in the shop is determined primarily by his relationships within the union. His authority depends on the collective bargaining agreement and he must be guided in his immediate job by union objectives. Questions were designed to find: (1) how well the union establishes its objectives; (2) whether the union representatives have the information needed to do their job; and (3) whether the shop relationships correspond to the ideas of top union and management officials.

Section 1 of Table 24 gives the answers in the first area. Of particular interest is the great stress laid on the bargaining relationship as a source of information about the company. Also interesting is the fact that while

TABLE 24. EXTENT TO WHICH UNION REPRESENTATIVES ARE INFORMED

			Per cent replying
1. Motives for joining union			
to get better wages and working conditions			90
to find out about management through bargaining			80
to get action on grievances			70
because it expressed the worker's views on national issues			40
because friends joined			20
		Per cent replying	
2. Knowledge of bargaining issues		*worked for*	*secured*
cost-of-living adjustment		95	50
basic wage increase		100	75
liberalized benefits		30	70
profit sharing plan		20	20
		Informed	
3. Information on job matters	*well*	*moderately*	*poorly*
about contract negotiations	91	9	—
about grievances	67	10	23
about job descriptions	86	4	10
about the rate committee	95	—	5
about scheduled changes	95	5	—
about promotions	86	14	—

the union does nothing actively about national issues, almost half of the representatives feel that it expresses their political views. Section 2 shows that the union representatives themselves are not fully informed in regard to immediate objectives and gains of the union. Only three-fourths of the executive committee members participating in the poll knew that the union had secured a basic wage increase and only half of them knew that a cost-of-living adjustment had been secured. There was more justification for confusion on benefits since the union has talked a great deal about benefits, although this subject is contractually not a bargainable issue. Profit sharing was never in the picture and yet a few executive board members thought it was a union demand. The striking fact emerges that the union representatives do not know with any degree of accuracy what the union has been seeking.

Several questions sought to analyze the internal means of union communications used to establish these objectives. All revealed that meetings are the heart of the system, with *Independent News and Views* as a secondary channel. For the union representatives, the executive board meeting is the primary means. However, their comments as a whole strongly support both membership and department meetings (70 per cent and 65 per cent respectively). Asked "In what ways do you feel the union has given you and your men more voice in matters affecting your jobs?", 75 per cent selected union meetings while 70 per cent chose union representatives. With meetings so important, it is noteworthy that in many departments they are irregular. In process departments, which are on shifts, a real problem arises that can be met only by holding small meetings. But even in the other departments a majority indicated that meetings are held only on special occasions.

Much of the specific information that is important to the steward or union representative in the performance of his job comes through meetings, usually the executive board meeting. Asked how they were informed of the effect of new contract provisions on their department, 10 mentioned the executive board meeting, 3 joint company and union meetings, 3 company meetings, and 6 other representatives or rumor. Replying similarly to a question on grievances, 10 stated they received information through the executive board meeting, 9 through rumors and other representatives. These results coupled with the evident lack of correct information on contract provisions would seem to indicate that channels for intra-union communications are not always well defined. These indications must be weighed against the general approval of the executive board meetings expressed by the union representatives, both as a means of expression and of communication. Nevertheless if the union is to live up to its goals of democracy and protection of employees' rights, substantial improvements in communications would appear desirable.

Section 3 of Table 24 shows the results of questions in the job area. Union representatives were asked whether they received information on six specific subjects related to their jobs. The replies would seem to indicate that in all matters except grievances information was felt to be satisfactory. However, the answers to several other questions require modifications in this conclusion. For example, 30 per cent of the union representatives felt that the men did not have an accurate knowledge of job descriptions, a feeling corroborated by the employee poll; and 33 per cent felt that they were not always given full explanations of the reasons for changes in work schedules. Nevertheless the general impression gained was that the union representatives considered themselves adequately informed to fulfill their responsibilities in the shop.

Shop relations, the third general area, were directly checked in a group of questions asked of both the union representatives and the foremen. These were designed to find out if the friendly relationship built between union and management at higher refinery levels persisted. Union representatives were asked whether the foreman passed on to them all information on company policy that was needed. Sixty per cent answered affirmatively, 27 per cent felt the information given was irregular and not dependable, and 13 per cent claimed that they were given information only on the highlights of policy. A second question asked the members of each group how well informed the other was on contract provisions and other matters of joint interest. The foremen gave the union representatives a high mark, 62 per cent rating them well informed, and 31 per cent more marking moderately well informed. The union representatives rated the foremen lower in this respect, only 15 per cent marking "well informed," 50 per cent indicating "moderately well informed," and 30 per cent choosing "often poorly informed." A final question sought to measure the freedom of exchange of information between foremen and stewards. Here 53 per cent of the foremen answering felt the exchange was free as compared to 45 per cent of the union representatives. Altogether these answers indicate that the union-management relationship at the shop level fails to a considerable extent to reflect the attitude of higher officials.

While the union representatives feel comparatively well informed in the areas of mutual interest, the weakness of the internal union communications would appear to deprive them of some of their effectiveness. Both management's desire to give the union a constructive place in the company, and the union's concern for representing the workers' interests at the local level, depend substantially on a well informed union organization. The response to the questionnaire indicates that much still remains to be done in order to achieve these objectives.

XI. EMPLOYEE REACTION

AN important test of the impact of organizational concepts and the system of communications which seeks to effectuate them is in the reaction of the employees of a company. Communications within Standard Oil are guided by three outstanding ideas: an understanding of company policy in its broadest aspects; a well defined sense of responsibility and authority within line management; and a constructive union relationship based on local needs. Previous chapters have dealt with the effectiveness of communications in establishing these objectives at various levels within the organization. Considerable attention has been paid to the operation of the superstructure because it is through this structure that the ideas are made effective. But it is at the employee level that the company and union objectives must be finally appraised and the communication system evaluated.

In order to make such an evaluation a questionnaire was given to 361 of the refinery's 3,800-odd employees. Questions were designed both to test knowledge in certain areas and to gather opinions relative to the existing methods of communication. The answers to these questions show in the first place that the average employee is concerned with overall company policy and would like to know better how his job relates to it; secondly, that for his immediate job needs, he depends on both his foreman and his representative according to the subject involved; and thirdly, although his detailed knowledge of the union objectives is somewhat limited, he gives the union considerable credit for improving his work situation and considers its existence important to him.

A. KNOWLEDGE OF POLICY

Employees were asked the same general questions about company history and overall manufacturing policy as were put to the foremen and stewards. Table 25 indicates that the trend of knowledge follows roughly the same pattern—considerable vagueness on general matters, more accuracy coupled with increased interest in financial matters, and most interest and knowledge where manufacturing policy comes home to the job in cost control. The company has exposed its employees to a fairly consistent barrage of publications—the *Esso Refiner*, the *Lamp*, the annual report, cost control posters, orientation and other material that give the employees through several media information on all the subjects covered by the questions. The conclusion would seem to be that where it is direct and pertinent the information makes a lasting impression; where it is not, it is apt to be passed over or forgotten quickly.

TABLE 25. EMPLOYEE KNOWLEDGE OF GENERAL COMPANY POLICY

	Percentage replying
1. Knowledge of refinery products	
correct	42
incorrect	58
2. Knowledge of company profits	
correct	56
too high	9
too low	9
don't know	26
3. Interest in company profits	
want to know more	92
don't want to know more	8
4. Purpose of cost control program*	
increase profits by cutting personnel	5
safeguard against diminishing demand	19
improve unit efficiency	76
provide funds for capital expansion	32
don't know	7

* In some cases, more than one item was checked.

Closer analysis shows that employees have least interest in the most general area. A question on affiliates not included in Table 25 produced only 12 per cent fully correct answers. The poor showing on refinery products must be weighed against the interest expressed about refinery operations in two write-in questions. Evidently it is not enough simply to make information of this kind available. Casual mention in the *Lamp* or the *Refiner*, both of which are well read, doesn't seem to have caught hold.

The better showing on the profits question reflects company and, to some extent, union efforts. The annual report distributed to all employees is a comprehensive document, and the union has also discussed profits in its newspaper and meetings. Despite this, only slightly over half of the employees answering named the correct figure. Asked how they had learned most about company finances, employees rated the *Lamp* first, the annual report second, the *Refiner* third, the newspapers fourth, and the union paper a poor fifth. The additional fact that 92 per cent of the employees indicated an interest in learning more about the company's financial policy would seem to indicate that the information now published is too remote. Surprisingly enough, employees made fewer errors in the cost control question than the foremen and indicated an almost equally high interest in knowing the efficiency of their units. Taken together these answers would seem to show that financial information, to be absorbed, must be tied directly to refinery problems.

Certain personnel policies are of greater interest to employees than overall manufacturing plans, or at least so the answers to the write-in question indicate.[1] However, knowledge of the details of personnel policy is not particularly accurate. Table 26 shows the replies to a question on principles and to two specific questions on the benefit program and on provisions of the union contract. Continual reiteration of the company's basic program combined with fairly consistent practice has clearly borne fruit. Only 7 per cent and 4 per cent of those responding marked as principles of the company the two items "limit unions where possible," and "hire executives from outside" that are not Esso policies. The greatest failure to identify existing company policy was in regard to career promotions, thus substantiating the foremen's opinion that the information given to employees on promotional opportunities was inadequate.

TABLE 26. EMPLOYEE KNOWLEDGE OF COMPANY PERSONNEL POLICY

	Percentage replying
1. Knowledge of principles of	
job stability	71
pay prevailing wage	71
personal security	60
full union recognition	52
career promotions	25
limit unions	7
hire executives from outside	4
2. Knowledge of benefit deductions	
correct	46
incorrect	54
3. Knowledge of contract provisions	
correct	20
incorrect	80

Less accurate knowledge was revealed in the replies to the detailed questions. Asked to select which of four security plans were paid for by a pay roll deduction, only 46 per cent selected the correct three. The predominant error made by 44 per cent was in holding that the survivor benefit plan was paid for by a deduction. Despite this, only 11 per cent expressed active dissatisfaction with company information on benefits and another 23 per cent moderate dissatisfaction. The few suggestions offered for improved information on benefit plans urged simpler literature and fuller explanations. The fact that such a large number were confused as to how plans are financed points up the practical need for following these suggestions. At present almost all the company booklets

[1] See Table 28, page 108.

are fairly detailed and full of legal terminology. Nowhere is there a simple statement of all the plans cutting through the constant revisions and financial involvements.

The statements related to the labor contract referred to the provision for voluntary arbitration of grievances not settled within the company, three weeks paid vacation for 15-year employees, and loss of seniority rights after a one year termination from the company. While only the vacation provision has caused any fanfare during the past three years, all of them are fairly significant clauses. Most of the answers were correct in regard to the vacation statement, with the errors falling almost equally between the other two. This can only suggest that even though the contract is widely distributed, it is not well understood. It would seem that the union has not made the most of explaining to the employees the part of policy that is jointly formulated.

B.   INFORMATION ON THE JOB

Satisfactory job performance is the direct or indirect objective of all communications. Policy may give the job its setting, but in the end the focus is on the actual operations involved in refining oil. Company officials, from the vice-president in charge of manufacturing to the line foremen, are charged with the responsibility for seeing that the job is done. The employee completes the chain. At the heart of the whole communications system therefore is the question of whether he receives adequate information to enable him or to encourage him to perform his job efficiently.

Within the shop the employee is in direct contact with the foreman and the steward. His interest in both of them stems from his work and they in turn are primarily concerned with matters that arise from his job. In appraising the effectiveness of communications on job matters, the first step is to see what the employee expects from the foreman and steward. Does his concept of responsibility correspond to the ideas of top officials? Once this is established the adequacy of job information and the areas where improvement is possible can be examined.

In Table 27, the answers to nine questions asking where an employee would go for additional information on specific subjects are tabulated. In them a fairly consistent trend is evident. The employee expects the foreman or other management representatives to have principal responsibility in matters concerned with schedules, department operations, training and promotions. In matters of rights or regulations he is expected to share his responsibility with the union steward. These findings match fairly closely the opinions of the foremen and union representatives recorded in the previous chapter.[1]

TABLE 27. EMPLOYEE OPINION AS TO SOURCES OF
INFORMATION ON SPECIFIC SUBJECTS

Subject	Source of Information			
	Percentage replying			
	Management[1]	Steward	Both	Other[2]
Schedule change	88	4	4	4
Department operation	81	7	8	4
Training	73	14	2	1
Reasons for changes	66	27	7	—
Promotions	70	24	4	2
Working rules	58	38	3	1
Job descriptions	53	36	10	1
Overtime rules	44	52	3	1
Personal grievances	24	68	4	4

[1] "Management" includes foremen, department heads, personnel department and publications put out by the company.

[2] "Other" includes mostly information from other employees.

It would thus appear that there is a fairly definite distinction of function in the employee's mind. This corresponds only in part to the distinction made at higher levels. The foreman has clear responsibility in carrying out the technical aspects of policy; the steward acts to interpret its effect upon the individual worker. From each, the employee expects information on immediate matters such as job descriptions, working and overtime rules, and to some extent the reasons for changes. Thus the emphasis placed by top management on establishing foremen responsibility in communications is well taken; but it seems equally important to insure that stewards are correctly apprised of activities in the shop. The significant point is that once the union is in the shop, a double line of communication develops on matters of shop interest. While the union has much of its motivation in areas apart from job performance, its agents are expected to know about immediate job matters. All this emphasizes the importance of insuring a good understanding of overall policy among both stewards and foremen, and establishing clearly the areas where mutual understanding is needed, if effective operation of the shop is to be achieved.

The remaining questions on job information were designed to find how well the system worked. Table 28 contains some of the results. In all areas a substantial number felt that matters had either been only partly explained or not explained at all. This compares with the fairly

[1] See page 96.

high degree of interest expressed in knowing the reasons why a job is assigned and in finding how well the department compares in efficiency with other departments.

TABLE 28. ADEQUACY OF JOB INFORMATION

		Percentage replying	
	Fully explained	*Partly explained*	*Not explained*
1. Type of Information			
Explanation of job duties	59	30	11
Reasons for changes	62	21	17
On opportunities	64	11	25
On training	55	16	29
Reason for assignment	53	28	19
	Want more information	*Unsure*	*Don't want more*
2. Worker interest in			
Reasons for job assignment	94	2	4
Department efficiency	81	11	8

Several points emerge in detailed analysis of these questions. The fact that 41 per cent have not received adequate explanations of their job duties is probably related to the fact revealed in another question that 55 per cent did not know job descriptions were available. Job descriptions have been rewritten recently, and each union steward will be given a copy for his men. Theoretically, written descriptions had previously been available through the foreman. In the area of opportunities and training, where employees showed a lack of understanding of company policy, only 30 per cent felt that insufficient training was available. It is even more surprising that so many were ignorant of the seniority agreement. Only 54 per cent realized that department service took precedence over company service in promotions. In interpreting these replies it must be remembered that many employees hold the same jobs for years and, with no particular prospect of advancement, are not especially interested in further training. However, the fact that "training and opportunities" rated highest when employees were given a chance to mention the subjects on which they desired more information (Table 31, 2) suggests the lack of information on promotional opportunities is a matter of real discontent among a substantial minority.

Employees reflected a general feeling that the company is interested in their ideas (91 per cent) and a wide acquaintance with the Coin Your Ideas Program. Further some 55 per cent thought that foremen were very willing to discuss such ideas, 25 per cent or more termed them moderately willing, and only 10 per cent thought they were actually unwilling. To a general question asking whether information was satisfactory in several areas over 80 per cent marked satisfactory in all cases with the lowest total appearing in the area of promotions. This reply ran about 20 per cent ahead of factual questions on the completeness of information received. Thus it would appear that although in some areas information on the job is actually quite weak and more is wanted, there is little real dissatisfaction.

C. THE FUNCTION OF THE UNION

To employees, the union appears as an important part of their environment in the company. Fifty-seven per cent selected improved union relations as the reason they received more information about the company, and, in the discussion of job information, the shop steward figured as a parallel source of information to the foreman in many areas. The union has thus had an effect which extends beyond its own immediate goals.

Several questions were designed to see how well employees understood the union objectives and whether they expected anything different from the union. These revealed a somewhat hazy knowledge of union purposes, particularly with regard to its most immediate bargaining points. A second group of questions took up the internal operation of the union. Answers to these revealed considerable informality of method and some dissatisfaction with the flow of information. Replies to several other questions indicated that the employees feel the foreman-steward relationship in the shop to be reasonably good.

In Table 29, answers to the two questions on union purposes are summarized. It is apparent that while the motives for joining the union

TABLE 29. MOTIVES OF UNION MEMBERSHIP AND
KNOWLEDGE OF OBJECTIVES

		Percentage replying	
1.	Reasons for Joining		
	to get better wages and working conditions	76	
	to learn more about management	50	
	to get action on grievances	49	
	because it expressed the worker's point of view	31	
	because friends joined	10	
		worked for	secured
2.	Immediate Union Goals		
	basic wage increase	82	58
	cost-of-living adjustment	84	83
	liberalized benefit program	57	35
	profit sharing plan	23	9

center about improved wages and working conditions they extend beyond this immediate objective. The union is in large measure a means of expression for employees. Half of those answering said they joined "to find out through bargaining what management was doing," and another 31 per cent felt that the union expresses their views on national issues, despite the fact that its leaders make no effort in this direction. Together with the frequent expression that the union has improved communications within the company, these replies point to the union as an organization of sentiment and opinion as well as for bargaining.

This idea is further supported by answers to the question on union objectives during the past year. While 83 per cent realized that the union had won a cost of living allowance, only 58 per cent knew that they had also secured a basic wage increase. As mentioned in Chapter X,[1] there was some justification for confusion on benefits since the union in its coalition meeting with top management did discuss benefits. A profit sharing plan has never been part of the union program. Thus a substantial minority evidently was not aware of the union's greatest achievement during the year, a large group gave credit to the union for benefits granted by the company, and a considerable number attributed to the union an objective it had never mentioned. Part of the blame for this lack of knowledge undoubtedly lies with imperfect union communications, but some would seem due to apathy that comes with comparatively satisfactory conditions.

The questions on internal communications within the union showed considerable weakness particularly in regard to collective bargaining meetings. As has already been indicated, this is the subject most employees want to know more about from the union. Asked "through what channels do you usually hear of contract negotiations," two-thirds selected the union representative, and about one-half the *Independent News and Views*. Less than a third mentioned meetings and about a quarter said daily newspapers. The irregularity with which the union paper is published and the comparatively poor showing of the union representatives on matters of fact would seem to explain much of the dissatisfaction.

The importance of the union paper and the union representative is emphasized in two questions about meetings. Fifty-eight per cent indicated that they attended meetings either irregularly (50 per cent) or never (8 per cent). To some extent this is due to the fact that too few meetings are held. However, attendance at meetings is a persistent prob-

[1] See page 100.

lem. Within the IPW those who miss meetings rely principally on their steward for information (67 per cent), almost half on the union paper, and 26 per cent on bulletin board announcements. Clearly these channels must be made more reliable if the membership is to be kept fully informed on union affairs.

Viewing union communications as a whole, employees expressed reasonable satisfaction both as to the information they receive and the opportunity they are given to express their views. Seventy-five per cent felt that the union kept them either fairly well informed (45 per cent), or well informed (30 per cent) of its activities, and over 80 per cent thought they had a chance to tell the union their ideas on bargaining issues. This would seem to indicate that from a practical point of view the union does function democratically although its machinery is far from perfect. Again the inference appears that the detailed facts of the union are less important than its actual existence in the eyes of the employees.

Within the shop, employees feel that their representative is willing to talk with them and is generally fairly well informed. Two-thirds termed their stewards very willing "to discuss suggestions and problems" and another 22 per cent thought that he was moderately willing. Somewhat less unanimity was expressed over the extent of information possessed by the stewards. Forty-two per cent considered him well informed and 32 per cent moderately well informed, while 17 per cent answered "knows little."

Employee opinion on union relations was quite similar to that expressed by foremen and stewards.[1] Fifty-four per cent chose the statement "foremen and union representatives exchange information only as required by the labor agreement" in preference to one specifying free exchange on all matters dealing with the work of the group. However, 64 per cent felt that the company's attitude toward the union was to "treat it fairly and seek its support in all matters affecting employees." Only 5 per cent said that the company sought to avoid dealings with the union whenever possible. Thus, in general, the union relation existing within the shop appears to be one that facilitates rather than retards the up and down movement of information.

Further it appears that the union leaders have interpreted the employees' attitude toward the union with accuracy and fitted the union into the company structure satisfactorily. Employees expect the union to act as their voice both in determining policy and in interpreting it at

[1] See page 93.

the shop level. The leaders' interest in union democracy and effective grievance machinery reflects these interests. Their efforts have been abetted by management's attitude of dealing with the union realistically at the bargaining table and recognizing its place in company affairs. This measure of success should not disguise the fact, however, that it takes continued positive action to maintain the relationship, and that weaknesses exist. Throughout the answers, contract negotiations showed up as the chief area in which more information was desired, and bargaining matters as the least well known.

D. EVALUATION OF MEDIA

Several questions were designed both to evaluate the media of communications used by the company and union in publicizing policy and to secure criticisms and suggestions. Answers to these questions revealed on the whole a high level of readership in the case of printed material, an almost equal dependence on written and spoken media, and considerable interest in more information related to matters of immediate concern.

Table 30 summarizes the results of the questions on readership. It shows in the first place that the company publications are much more consistently read than the union, and secondly that publications do form a fairly reliable base for policy communications to employees. Of some interest is the high readership accorded to the *Lamp*, a typographically impressive magazine carrying serious articles on the oil industry. The thrift plan statement quite naturally commands attention since it deals

TABLE 30. EXTENT TO WHICH PUBLICATIONS ARE READ BY EMPLOYEES

	Percentage replying		
1. Current Publications	read regularly	read occasionally	don't read
Esso Refiner	95	5	—
The Lamp	73	21	6
bulletin board	63	23	14
Independent News & Views	50	20	30
2. Booklets*		read	keep
safety booklet		93	82
thrift plan annual statement		84	65
working rules		76	54
benefit booklets		74	61
company annual report		57	19
Your Job		54	35
union contract		52	38
union constitution		50	38

* Many marked both read and keep.

with the employees' personal funds. The low rating for the labor contract and the union constitution accords with the low level of understanding of contract provisions.

Comments on the *Refiner* were generally favorable. The replies indicate that all features are well read, running from promotions, read by
83 per cent, to want ads, read by 65 per cent, with high ratings given
editorials and personals. "A bigger and more local paper" was the most
frequent suggestion offered, with interest divided about equally between
more refinery and more personal news. Sentiment for more frequent
publication predominated in the comments concerning *Independent News
and Views*. Employees count on the paper for news of recent union
activities (65 per cent) and for editorial opinion, but many indicated
that it was hard to get hold of and others felt that it was run to too great
extent by the already overburdened union officers.

Other information on attitudes towards media was obtained in the
more general questions about company and union communications. In
the first group, employees were asked which of six suggested means they
thought the company and the union should adopt to keep them better
informed, and in the second, subjects they would like to learn more about
from the company and the union. Tables 30 and 31 show the results of
these questions.

All company methods received about equal support. This would seem
to indicate that the company program is at present fairly well balanced.

TABLE 31. EMPLOYEE SUGGESTIONS FOR IMPROVED COMMUNICATIONS
FROM MANAGEMENT

	Percentage replying
1. Suggested methods	
more information in the *Refiner*	53
more meetings with supervisors	50
more information to union	49
more information on bulletin boards	49
better informed supervisors	48
more training courses	45
2. Suggested subjects*	
training and opportunities	39
benefits and protection	19
refinery operations	16
business operations	10
bargaining policy	8
personnel policy	6
about my job	6

* 132 employees answered the question "What subjects would you like to learn more
about from the company?"

TABLE 32. EMPLOYEE SUGGESTIONS FOR IMPROVED COMMUNICATIONS
FROM THE UNION

		Percentage replying
1.	Suggested methods	
	more factual reports on bargaining	70
	more information on bulletin boards	56
	more department meetings	53
	more information in the union paper	52
	more membership meetings	23
	more union training courses	20
2.	Suggested subjects*	
	more about relations with company	42
	other jobs and advancement	26
	business dealings and activities	17
	contract provisions	6
	benefit plans	6
	labor legislation	4
	outside union activities	2

* 115 employees answering "What subjects would you like to know more about from the union?"

The increased use of the *Refiner* and bulletin boards rated with more meetings and better informed supervisors. Almost equal support was shown for more information through union channels. The considerable interest in more training courses, which had already been noted, was most pronounced in answers to the open-end question. Such interest in self-betterment contrasts with the small number (25 per cent) who knew correctly the company policy on career promotion.

In regard to communications from the union, answers both to the question on methods and to the one on subjects showed a predominant interest in details of union-management relations. It is noteworthy that no printed summaries of bargaining sessions were available to employees other than as printed intermittently in the *Independent News and Views*. Small meetings were preferred over large ones, with particular stress on more department meetings, which were held only irregularly. The greatest interest was in the area of fundamental union activities. Employees want to know what the union is bargaining over with management.

While the improvement of specific media is unquestionably important in building a communications system, the background relationship cannot be overlooked. Two-thirds of the employees felt they were now receiving more information than when they began work with the company, but only 11 per cent mentioned publications as the reason and 6 per cent more the personnel department, supervisory training, or the orientation program. Over half specified either the union (30 per cent), the company attitude (13 per cent), or improved labor-management relations (11 per cent), while 18 per cent felt their own experience had made the difference. Thus it would appear that the employees feel that satisfactory communications depend primarily on the conditions existing in the company rather than on specific media used. The first requirement is that the willingness should be there, and the union apparently stands as a symbol in assuring this willingness.

XII. REVIEW OF FINDINGS OF
CASE STUDY TWO

FROM the detailed study of communications at each level within the Esso Standard Oil Company emerges a picture of the environment in which union and management programs operate. The study took as its point of departure the proposition that communications should be appraised in terms of the organization as a whole. It examined the communication system both as it was related to the accomplishment of the company's business and as it affected the interests of management and the union. This overall approach pointed up the fundamental differences in the motives of the two parties but at the same time stressed the areas of mutuality in their communications objectives and activities.

A. OBJECTIVES OF COMMUNICATIONS

1. *Management's view*

No two of the approximately 20 executives interviewed mentioned exactly the same objectives for management's communication efforts. In general, however, the executives involved in policy development stressed broader aims, and those nearer the employees the need for more specific information. The former saw most clearly the need for understanding of policies as a basis for favorable attitudes. If every member of management understood the company's philosophy of corporate responsibility and fair dealing in employee relations, they would, it was felt, be well prepared to effectuate policies uniformly in their daily organizational duties. Both of these philosophies have been repeated over and over in training courses and printed material. Lower management tends to take them for granted, but upper management sees the need to keep the entire organization fully aware of the implications of these policies to day-to-day operational problems.

Next to creation of favorable attitudes, management as a whole gave most emphasis to the value of communications in strengthening the principle of managerial responsibility. In accord with this principle, individual executives are given a maximum of independence in guiding the operations for which they are responsible. This independence must, however, be based on an understanding of policies and frequent consultation on objectives. Communication is, thus, vital to the effectuation of this principle.

The third broad objective of communications in Esso, and the one ranked highest by department heads, was the development of an informed working force. This meant a reasonably adequate understanding of company objectives and philosophy, knowledge of specific plans for the department, and an idea of how these plans affect the individual at work. Esso executives, imbued with the philosophy of managerial responsibility, believe that supervisors and employees do their best work when they have the sense of security afforded by policies consistently applied and advance information on what is expected of them.

2. *The role of the union*

The union's concern with communications is principally in the upward flow from employees to management. Channeling the employees' point of view to management through collective bargaining or the grievance procedure is part and parcel of the union's basic function—to improve the employees' status. While the union leaders' comments gave less emphasis to the union's role in the downward flow of information, it was clear that they accepted this as both the right and the duty of the union.

The fact that collective bargaining at the Bayway refinery is conducted on a friendly, factual basis and with little competition for the employees' loyalty is an important element in setting the pattern for management and union communications with each other and with the employees. Management looks upon the union as the principal channel for communicating with and informing the worker. As a result the content of communications deals more with matters of common interest than with matters of conflict. The union does not fail to present to its members its differences with management, but these are more often presented as different interpretations of factual data than as aggressive statements against management.

The Independent union's participation in the coalition committee apparently was looked upon more as a broadening of sources of information than as an extension of bargaining. Moreover, from the time of the union's establishment, management had given information voluntarily on many developments outside the scope of bargaining. Thus objectives in Esso not only tend to make collective bargaining an important part of communications, but also to make communications between management and the union considerably broader than the present bargaining area.

B.   EFFECTIVENESS OF COMMUNICATIONS

Both management and the union have designed their informational efforts with the idea of building up worker participation. The reaction of individuals at all levels indicates, first, that their primary interest is in matters connected with their jobs and, second, that both management and union channels are generally effective in influencing attitudes, if not always successful in transmitting detailed information.

1. *The importance of securing understanding of policy within top management*

At the top level within the New York offices of the parent company and of Esso Standard, the problem is to develop policy in terms of the whole organization. The principal resource is an extensive meeting system. Broad policies are explained directly to and discussed with the men responsible for carrying them out. The company has sought through a system of meetings and personal consultation to avoid the dangers of policies determined and enforced from above. In the area of manufacturing plans, it has achieved considerable success: its policies are understood and individuals have well established means of recourse in cases of misunderstanding. In the area of personnel policy the situation appears less satisfactory: the general outline of policy is approved centrally, with details worked out and administered according to the needs of the local situation. This has resulted in some confusion among management personnel and in the union demand for information from the central authority. There appears to be need for clarification as to the point of decision, and then careful channeling of information from this point to all parties concerned.

2. *The problem of resolving local viewpoints with top policy*

Company and union communication policies have a direct impact in the refinery. The refinery officials must operate within the general scheme of organization and operations finally decided at a higher level. Their reactions indicate general satisfaction with the subject matter presented and with the allocation of responsibility. In matters related to the business, interest is naturally geared to refinery needs, but not solely. On the whole both the company and the union officials want to be well acquainted with those parts of company policy that have a direct bearing on their work in the refinery. Some concern is expressed about the presentation of the refinery management point of view to the New York executive group, particularly in the area of personnel policy. The union has sought information directly from the New York office, and a number of executives expressed the opinion that upward communications through all levels were not as satisfactory as the downward flow. The Esso management operates on the basis of pooled judgments, making special provision for group and personal contacts between the various levels of management. The fact that, even with such special arrangements, upward communications are felt by some executives to give top management an inadequate picture of local problems suggests the inherent difficulties in two-way communications in any large organization.

3. *The need for precise definition of authority within the refinery*

The definitions of managerial and union authority worked out against the total company picture are followed quite closely in the refinery. The idea of managerial responsibility is overwhelmingly approved. The few difficulties reported appeared to be due in part to unclear lines of authority, in part to the newness of the concept of individual responsibility, and in part to incomplete definition of the limits of responsibility. Similarly in the collective bargaining relation there remains some lack of precision. The union function will probably become clearer as more bargaining experience has accumulated. The significant fact at the moment is that management recognizes the union's place and is seeking to build a relationship based on the performance of definite tasks.

4. *The interest in knowing why at the shop level*

Shop relations reveal most clearly the workings of company and union communication policies. Foremen and union representatives alike wanted to know the whys of various directives they have had to carry out or explain. They were concerned with getting information, both to satisfy their own curiosity and to answer the direct questions of the employees. In the matter of media, there was, as at higher levels, a wide reliance on direct person-to-person methods, especially in regard to shop practice. But written publications and memoranda were important media in gaining an understanding of policy. When it came to saying why communications had improved, there was general agreement that it was a matter of attitudes and institutions more than methods. The important attitudes for supervisors and stewards were the desire to know and willingness to communicate. Of outstanding interest to the workers was the provision of an acceptable guaranty of reliability in the independent union, rather than an elaboration of techniques.

5. *The common interest of foremen and steward in communications*

The line between the areas of management and union responsibility in keeping employees informed is not clear cut. At one extreme, the foremen are generally conceded to have responsibility for operating information; at the other, the union is given principal responsibility in the area of employee rights. But in between there is a considerable area of common concern, matters on which it is important for both to have accurate information. In developing the foreman's authority, the training courses provide an excellent background. But more important to the functioning of the shop is regular provision of information on all matters with which he must deal. Also it is evident that, despite management's intentions, a considerable amount of by-passing does occur. On the union side, representatives do not appear to have adequate information about union activities. While they claim considerable responsibility for themselves, they indicate that reports on many matters reach them only irregularly. Moreover, their understanding of fundamental union policy is vague and incomplete. Interchange of information between foremen and stewards is on a fairly friendly basis. However the effectiveness of both might be improved through more distinct division of responsibility and the development of means of assuring that both groups are fully and accurately informed.

6. *The dependence of employees on both management and union sources*

The employee reaction to communications within the Esso Bayway refinery shows a keen interest in knowing about the company, and dependence on both management and union channels for this information. Thus it would appear that the overall communication policy is well conceived. But in the details of the employee response, certain soft spots appear. In the area of company background, employees want more specific information on the things they are doing, less general information on the company as a whole. When it comes to a discussion of profits, they are evidently not satisfied with the traditional balance sheet approach. The details of personnel policy do not seem as important as the general principles. What appears most important is the atmosphere in which information is made available. This is brought out by the emphasis placed on the union as the most important factor in improving communications, rather than on specific media.

For information on the job, employees rely on both foremen and stewards with some gradation of emphasis. The important fact is that for much information the two sources are interchangeable. Throughout, a substantial minority reported failure to obtain adequate information on direct job matters, although relatively little dissatisfaction. As for the union, employees measured its effectiveness in terms of their own jobs.

They were less concerned with its general objectives than with the increased confidence that having an organization of their own gave them. In the eyes of the employees, failures in internal union communications are apparently more than offset by the general improvement that the union has brought in the frank flow of information on all matters.

XIII. GENERAL SUMMARY AND CONCLUSIONS

THE approach to the study of communications in the Esso Standard Oil Company and in Johnson & Johnson was direct and pragmatic. The aim was to discover what actually constituted "communications," to trace the channels which were used, and to evaluate the effectiveness of union and management communications. Research covered, in addition to background information on each situation: the objectives of those in authority who determine what shall be told and how; experience with different channels and media; the reaction of the intermediate personnel and employees to the kind, amount, and timing of the information.

A study of two situations cannot pretend to offer a definitive answer to the question of what makes "good communications." As stated in the introduction, the two concerns were approached as separate and distinct situations. Little effort was made to handle the two studies in such a way that the communication systems and their effectiveness could be compared item by item. Nevertheless, the findings reveal certain elements common to successful efforts in communications. Taking into full account the backgrounds of the two cases, other organizations seeking improved understanding among executives and rank and file may find the reported experience of help.

A. MAJOR SIMILARITIES AND DIFFERENCES IN THE TWO SITUATIONS

Considered as a whole, the New Brunswick plants of Johnson & Johnson and the Bayway refinery of the Esso Standard Oil Company are markedly different in size, product, and organization. Considered in terms of communication, fundamental differences still exist, but the two situations have many points in common. The most evident and perhaps the most significant similarities were the efforts of all parties concerned to maintain peaceful and constructive union-management relations, and the recognition of the importance of satisfactory communications to the total operation of the plant or refinery.

More specific similarities of background, objectives, and methods of communications also existed. Three particular conditions in the background that may have influenced communications were: (1) while the area of study involved one or more units of a multiplant company, in both cases the units studied were closely associated with the top centralized administration; (2) both companies were concerned with the maintenance of clearly defined organizations and recognized the interdependence of sound organization and satisfactory communications; and (3) the companies each dealt only with one union in bargaining covering the particular units studied, and each of these unions was primarily a business union. Several similarities in company informational objectives were clear: (1) both concerns sought to secure throughout their organization as complete understanding as possible of company policies and reasons behind the policies; (2) both wanted to make their supervisors and employees generally aware of the economic problems of the business, and specifically to make them "cost conscious"; and (3) both hoped to prevent the spread of false rumors by giving out accurate and timely information.

In methods, the outstanding points in common were the use of the line organization as the core of communications and the acceptance of the union as of equal importance with the line organization in getting certain types of information to and from the employees. The communication systems of the two unions and managements revolved to a marked degree around meetings. Both companies have used printed media extensively and have issued periodically, or as occasion warranted, publications commonly considered to be the principal tools of an informational program, i.e. employee magazines, handbooks, annual reports, and supervisory manuals. But in spite of the fairly elaborate printed media, company executives stressed their greater reliance upon direct individual contact and meetings to gain understanding among management personnel, and upon personal relationships among the first-line supervisors, union representatives, and the employees to gain understanding among the rank and file. The two unions, with limited funds for printed materials, put even more stress upon person-to-person contacts.

The most fundamental differences between the two situations were in size, in competitive conditions in their product markets, in the longer history of the formal personnel program at Esso, and in the type of union. The larger corporation, with its many levels of management between the worker and the top policy-forming group, had the more complex communication problem. The greater competition and changing demands for its products facing Johnson & Johnson, as well as its position in a smaller industrial community, undoubtedly influenced management's outlook and tended to give its informational objectives in employee relations a public relations slant.

Although the two unions studied are predominantly business unions, seeking to get as much as possible for their members within the present

economic system, there are distinct differences between the CIO-affili-
ated Textile Workers and the Independent Petroleum Workers. The
effects of the longer-established personnel program at Esso and of the
attitude of the Independent Petroleum Workers are so closely related
that it is impossible to separate them into cause and effect. In any case,
the attitude of the union leaders at Esso was generally one of approval
of the personnel standards established by management long before the
union was organized. The Textile Workers, Local 630, in contrast,
feared that an elaborate personnel program might influence the loyalty
of the employees towards management and away from the union. The
Independent Petroleum Workers tended to view their role in communications as that of interpreting policies to employees and channeling
employee thinking to management. Local 630 considered such functions
to be only part of its responsibilities in communicating with its members.
Besides seeking to build a union with greater bargaining strength, the
Textile Workers had objectives in communications outside the work
situation. Some of these were different from management's objectives,
but not opposed to them; other differences carried seeds of conflict that
might lie dormant or grow, according to the climate of collective bargaining.

With these differences in background, it would have been surprising
had there not been some differences in objectives and methods. As mentioned above, Johnson & Johnson management viewed good employee
relations and good public relations as an almost indivisible goal in their
informational program. Top management also was concerned with safe-
guarding the system of free enterprise both by precept and example.
The Esso refinery management felt that good employee relations were
gained in the work situation rather than in the public forum and consequently tried to "make practice speak for itself." In a total consideration
of the viewpoints of the two companies, it must be noted that public
relations may have been given less prominence in the thinking of the
Esso Standard executives interviewed because much of this activity is
handled by the parent company. Although the expressed aim at all levels
of Esso was to demonstrate the benefits of free enterprise rather than to
talk about it, the difference between the attitudes of Esso and Johnson &
Johnson appeared to be principally one of degree.

B.   COMMON FACTORS IN SUCCESSFUL COMMUNICATIONS

In considering what appear to be elements strengthening communications in the two situations studied, one fact should be kept in mind: the
desire of both unions and managements to maintain friendly labor rela-

tions insofar as these were consistent with the fundamental objectives of the individual organization. Intra-company and intra-union communications might well assume very different aspects if conflict rather than peaceful relations were the objective of either party.

The findings of the two studies might be used to substantiate or disprove various hypotheses in regard to communications. No such attempt is made in these conclusions. The four principal factors discussed below were evident in the communications that went on in the Esso refinery and Johnson & Johnson plants as a part of industrial operations or other organizational activity. They are felt to be of practical significance in any attempts to improve communications in a situation where employees are organized.

1. Clearly defined lines of responsibility and authority

Both companies recognized the importance of clearly defined lines of responsibility and authority to satisfactory communications. Yet certain soft spots in informational channels appeared to be the result of weaknesses in the line organization. At the Bayway refinery, for instance, the most dissatisfaction with information received within the management group was expressed in departments least directly related to the central management of the refinery. At Johnson & Johnson, there were substantial indications that a reorganization of management functions a few years prior to the study had been an important factor in improved communications among management personnel. Acceptance of the inseparability of organization, operations, and communications are, both studies indicate, essential to the effective use of communications for improved operation.

In addition to the basic need for clear lines of responsibility and authority, three points in the impact of organization on communications are worthy of note.

a.   Formal channels of communications can be strengthened by coordination with informal channels.

Direct person-to-person exchange of information and points of view was felt by the individual members of management, by the union officers, and by employees to be most satisfactory. Sometimes this exchange was in a direct line relationship, sometimes it was not. Meetings were of particular help in incorporating this informal exchange into the established channels. At the employee level, posted bulletins were valued as a means of getting exact information on matters that might be more fully discussed by the supervisor or sometimes also disseminated by rumor.

b.   By-passing should be avoided if possible.

By-passing, which violates the principle of organizational responsibility, was found to create resentment among the individuals affected and also to lessen their feeling of responsibility for keeping their subordinates informed. In both companies, some evidence of by-passing was seen. The effort to get word to an individual or a particular group quickly, or the need to discuss a subject with the individual most concerned, sometimes resulted in conscious or thoughtless failure to use the line organization or to inform intermediate levels. The problem was how to maintain the line organization as an effective functioning channel, and yet not to allow it to slow up action seriously nor to prevent the informal consultations between staff and line and union and supervisors which were felt to be an important part of understanding.

c.   Staff departments can be used to strengthen the effectiveness of both formal and informal channels.

In both managements studied and in the Textile Workers Union, staff personnel helped substantially in the spread of information in printed form and by word of mouth. Although the Independent Petroleum Workers had little staff assistance, members of the Executive Committee serving as a subcommittee on research to some extent doubled in a staff capacity.

Both companies believed in using staff to strengthen the line rather than to assume line responsibilities. In the Esso refinery, technical staffs were an important element in the meetings system, as well as the principal source of technical explanation of changes in policies or operations. The personnel departments of both companies were especially concerned with the maintenance of clear lines of communications. They have served as eyes and ears for management in observing weaknesses in communications, and have considered it their responsibility to make specific recommendations looking towards improvement.

2. Attitudes that encourage a free exchange of information throughout the organization

Communications from upper to lower levels within most groups involve principally an effort by the higher level to influence the lower. Even in organizations as concerned with communications as Esso Standard Oil Company and Johnson & Johnson, and following as democratic procedures as the two unions studied, emphasis in actual communications was downward rather than upward. The following points appear to be important in the development of an atmosphere conducive to a free upward and downward exchange of information:

a.   If past attitudes have tended to limit the amount of information given out, part of the current program must concern itself with securing a recognition of the new policy in respect to communications.

While publications, such as handbooks and periodicals, are apparently helpful in gaining goodwill, the individual employee or member of management judges the willingness to communicate principally by his ability to get answers to questions or by the fullness of explanation given concerning changes in his work situation. The immediate supervisor should be trained promptly to reflect changes in top management attitudes.

b.   Success in imparting information is affected by a willingness to listen as well as to talk.

The individual, whether a member of management, a union representative, or an employee likes not only to be kept informed but also to be given a chance to ask questions or to comment on the information. He likes to feel also that his needs are considered when policies or operational plans are being developed. The two studies showed some feeling among the members of lower and middle management that they were reasonably well informed but that their points of view were not always represented or understood in top-management councils. The existence of the feeling among lower executives and union representatives that their particular needs were not given adequate attention, even in these organizations with systems of meetings at all levels, suggests that this problem is likely to assume serious proportions in organizations where opportunities for regular discussion between various levels are almost nonexistent.

c.   Fear of authority may act as a block to upward and downward communications.

The fact that the employees of both companies felt that communications had improved after unionization suggests that the rank and file gain a stronger sense of being "in the know" when their own elected representatives have access to upper management. Some evidence of respect for authority to the extent of failing to present their own or their employees' points of view to higher levels, even though there was easy access to their superiors, was also found in interviews with management first-line supervisors and union shop stewards. This fear, existing even in a minor degree, may prevent important attitudes from getting through to top management, and, in turn, prevent management and union officers from presenting their messages most realistically.

3. *Recognition of the interrelationships of*
management and union communications

The aims of the communication efforts of union or company were seen in both cases to be in terms of improving the effectiveness of the organization. Friendly inter-organizational relationships evidently required adequate and easy exchange of information throughout the various levels, but the final test of effectiveness of communications was felt to be in their impact upon the employee. In both situations, employees showed a desire to receive information from both the employer and the union. They recognized to a considerable extent the generally accepted areas of responsibility, but their answers also revealed many overlapping areas.

In the Johnson & Johnson study, where questions asked gave the employees an opportunity to indicate a preference in choice of information, they showed a definite liking for joint presentation on a number of subjects. On first reflection, this employee desire for joint presentation would seem to indicate a need for much closer coordination of management's and union's informational programs than was found in either situation. Conditions that prevented more extensive coordination were in some instances weaknesses that could be corrected. These included the failure of department heads and supervisors to understand and reflect top management's policy on collective bargaining, and confusion as to the responsibilities of foreman and shop steward in keeping the employee informed. More fundamental obstacles were the differing objectives of union and management, and union dissatisfaction with information received from management when bargaining was conducted at a level below that at which policy was determined.

The only conclusion which can be drawn from these two cases is that communications may be improved by recognition and clarification of the roles of both parties in keeping employees well informed, but that only limited coordination is practical. The considerations which follow appear to be important to the attainment of even a limited coordination.

a.   The total framework within which communications are carried on must be taken into account.

It was apparent in both studies that the organization and objectives of both the company and the union affected their individual planning as to what was to be told, how, and to whom. The type and education of individuals predominating in the group, the information previously given out, the ability of supervisors and shop stewards, and company and union community relations, as well as the relationship between the two organizations, were items that affected the planning. Failure to consider important parts of the background situation had resulted in a few instances not only in wasted effort but also in unexpected and unfavorable repercussions.

b. Management acceptance of the importance of the union in communications with employees is an essential element.

The managements in the two situations had accepted fully the union's interest, not only in being kept posted on what management told the employees, but also in being the principal channel for telling them. The employee attitude towards sources of information suggested that both supervisors and shop stewards should be well informed on all matters affecting the employee at work.

c. The union must be willing and able to fulfill its responsibility as a major channel of information.

Both unions took for granted their roles as the chief means of transmitting employee grievances and attitudes to management. They also felt strongly that they should be informed on matters directly or indirectly affecting collective bargaining and be given a chance to give the information to the employees from the union's point of view. Their ability to do the best possible job in communications was limited by lack of funds for extensive printed materials, by poorly trained shop stewards, and by poor attendance at membership meetings.

Although the employees gave their unions principal credit for improved communications in the plant, both groups of employees also showed considerable criticism of the union's informational efforts. This, as was suggested by some of the union officers, may have been an "intra-family" type of criticism which in no way affected an employee's loyalty to the union. It was felt, on the contrary, that if management were to try to take advantage of the union's weakness in this function it would be resented deeply by the employees. Both managements sought to avoid even the appearance of such an attempt. However, they felt that it was management's responsibility to make sure that certain information was available to the worker, and they often gave information to the union and supervisors almost simultaneously.

d. The first-line representatives of union and management must be well informed and willing and able to transmit information.

As noted above, the shop stewards were an important link in the union's channel of communications. The foremen were an equally important link on the management side. The free flow of information between union and management, and between both of them and the employee, depended to a large extent upon these key men in the shop. In both situations the foremen and stewards counted themselves of less importance in the informational chain than did their superiors or the employees. A considerable number of foremen were not sure of management's policy in collective bargaining and attitude toward the union, and a number of stewards were poorly informed on the aims of the union. It was apparent in both cases that a clearer understanding by foreman and steward of the basic aims of their respective organizations, and of their responsibility in interpreting these aims, would materially improve communications in the shop.

e.   Recognition of the common interest as well as the duality in management and union communications is important.

The mutuality and duality of management and union objectives in communications are almost inseparable from their objectives and functions in collective bargaining. It is worth noting that in the situation where the union had the broader and more independent objectives management showed the greater concern for emphasizing the mutual and common interests in educational and informational efforts. The union was willing to go along only to a certain point. Maintenance of a strong position for independent action was felt, for instance, to be of more importance than a joint educational program.

An understanding of the points of common and separate interest of the two organizations in getting the facts to employees was, it was evident, an element in successful planning in both situations studied. Information on subjects within the scope of collective bargaining was channeled through the union or through both management and the union. Information on scheduling, product changes, quality standards, production costs, and similar matters was management's responsibility in each case. Yet they were also often of direct concern to the worker and thus to his union. It was in matters of daily operation that the two managements felt the importance of using the line organization as the principal channel of communication with the workers, while also keeping the union fully informed in advance of notice to the employees. In such matters, communications were of considerable importance in maintaining the delicate balance of interests of management, union, and employee.

The two managements' concern with keeping their own executives informed and the unions' concern with their shop representatives also fell to some degree within the area of common interest.

There were indications that certain areas of interest to one party alone and of no apparent concern to the other might prove to have an indirect effect upon union-management relations. Management's efforts to use communications to weld together an efficient management group were looked upon with favor by union and employee. Political teaching by either side, when there were direct differences of opinion, was viewed with misgiving.

Certainly no rules can be laid down concerning the optimum emphasis on matters of common or independent interest. However, the considerable success in strengthening certain mutual efforts for improved communications in the two cases suggests one principle: that substantial common efforts can be developed only along with a complete recognition of the dual and independent functions of both parties.

4. Effective techniques

Specific methods of communication are of less fundamental significance to satisfactory understanding of common purposes within an organization than is an acceptance of the basic concept of communication as a problem of organization. Yet ways and means are by no means unimportant. Well planned methods of communication were used in both situations to keep the organization functioning smoothly. Although both companies gave more than average attention to methods, the findings of the two studies suggest certain problems likely to be faced by any group in developing satisfactory procedures. In broad terms, the principal technical aspects deserving consideration are:

a.   The selection for each specific subject of the most effective media or channels.

There were many evidences that for most subjects the use of only one channel or one medium of communication was inadequate. For example, the handbooks describing insurance, pension, and benefit plans were important means of getting full details to the employees, but a personal explanation by the supervisor or the staff handling these activities was necessary in connection with any direct application of a benefit plan to an individual employee. The lack of accurate knowledge of many of the workers of both companies suggested the need for giving information repeatedly through several media.

The reading habits of employees indicated that managements could count on a wide reading of the employee magazines. But whatever particular written media, pictographs, or movies are used to get a message directly to the employees, both managements accepted the importance of supplementing the impersonal media by personal explanation of supervisor, steward, or both. The two unions, limited by financial considerations in the amount of printed material they could distribute, leaned heavily on personal channels, and felt that these were far better than printed media in matters that really counted.

b.   The need to write or speak in terms understood by the group.

The employees of both the Esso Bayway refinery and the Johnson & Johnson plants, when given a chance to make their own comments, asked that certain subjects be explained in simpler language. Descriptions of benefit plans and clauses of the labor agreements, apparently, were not understood by many of the workers to whom they applied. Johnson & Johnson, recognizing this problem, had issued "Here's How" versions of their contracts, and both companies were seeking simpler and more effective ways of presenting other information.

c.   The need to present broad subjects in terms of the personal interest of the individual supervisor, steward, or worker.

If a message which must pass through several levels is to be delivered with accuracy and conviction, the individuals who pass the word along must not only understand the message but must have considerable interest in it. Evidence of this problem was found in supervisory failure to reflect accurately top management's attitude towards collective bargaining, and supervisory comment in regard to management's failure to understand their problems. The message also must have some personal meaning for the final recipient, if it is to make any lasting impression. Employees, for instance, showed a very uncertain acquaintance with facts presented in the annual report and repeated in other publications.

This problem is closely related to the organizational need of two-way communication. The people at the top who determine the policy, and the way in which it is to be explained, cannot do either with the optimum satisfaction to everyone affected unless they have some appreciation of the varying interests and needs of the different groups, and take these needs and interests into account in presenting policy or factual information. The attitude of the supervisor and steward means more to the employee than any message from higher levels. No matter how well phrased in writing, the content of a message is accepted largely in terms of the explanation or interpretive action of the supervisor or steward.

d.   The value of participation in gaining understanding.

To gain wide participation in development of policies and plans requires positive encouragement of ideas as well as a willingness to listen. Information moving upward or downward may be in the form of written messages, personal statements, or orders without discussion. Resulting action may be response without understanding and, possibly, with resentment. Executive and supervisory interest in meetings showed the great importance of thorough discussion to satisfactory communication within management levels.

The feeling of the employees of both companies that the amount of information given to them had been increased with the entrance of the union may have been in part the result of a sense of participation, as well as representation of their point of view through the union. Employee knowledge of union objectives was seen to have a high correlation with attendance at meetings. Those employees who did not know facts made available to them in print often believed that the management or the union had not given them this information. Thus it appeared that failure to participate not only resulted in less absorption of facts but, in a few instances, in a feeling of resentment at not being informed. Small attendance at union meetings suggests that workers need more than the opportunity to participate. They need to be convinced that participation offers more in personal satisfaction than it costs in effort expended.

The findings of both studies indicate that organization-wide understanding is hard to gain. The lack of knowledge on many subjects which management or the union had assumed the employees understood suggests that the organizations had accepted an uncritical attitude as proof of understanding. This implication of the two studies highlights the need for more careful consideration of methods of communications which can, *in the process of communicating*, test the degree to which the recipient *understands* what he is being told. In particular, it suggests the need of bringing the lowest levels of the management and the union more fully into the series of meetings which have proved to be an effective means of communication among upper management and union executive personnel.

The two on-the-spot studies have shown the difficulty of the task of transmitting information and ideas. They have also suggested the limitations in knowledge and understanding which may exist even among the executives, employees, and members of organizations following the practice of sharing information at all levels. Perhaps, most of all, these studies reveal the complex relationships involved in communications in industry, and the need for taking these relationships into full account in any informational planning aimed at cooperative action through understanding.

APPENDIX A

JOHNSON & JOHNSON
GUIDING RULES FOR COMMUNICATIONS[1]

General

1. All people on the management level must know the value and importance of communications.

2. All people in management must themselves be informed if they are to carry out their own responsibilities for communications.

3. Every action of any executive must include planning for communications as well as for other details. (For example, in replacing a man it is not enough to write a job description and job specification, recruit candidates, and interview and evaluate them. An executive must also determine who the affected parties are, what shall be told them, how it shall be told, by whom and when.)

4. The most difficult thing in communications is determining who will be affected by an event and, therefore, who should be told. This requires that mature, stable and successful people, usually well up in management, put themselves in the shoes of others who are less secure and judge what the latter need and want to know.

The Timing of Communications

1. Timing should be such that a supervisor always hears information before his subordinates.

2. All persons on any level who receive information for passing on must share a responsibility for passing it on as nearly simultaneously and uniformly as possible.

3. If it is decided to inform people about any event, the informing should take place well in advance of rumors, gossip and conjectures. If the information deals with vacations, shutdowns, etc., it should be released soon enough to be useful to individuals whom it was intended to benefit.

4. All announcements should be timed so that the reasons given for them do not have any chance of conflicting with other information fresh in employees' minds. (The employment of outside consultants to study the need for a revised plant layout was announced on a bulletin board on the same day that employees were informed by bulletin that there were to be layoffs due to lack of sales.)

---

[1] These "Guiding Rules" were developed at Johnson & Johnson after the communication study described in Case One was made. They were prepared by a committee and revised after being tried out in executive and supervisory conferences. While the principle of having such guiding rules as a basis for action is definitely accepted, the statement is considered to be experimental and in no sense final.

Who Should Be Told?

1. If one person in a department or in a unit is told, all who are equally in need of the information must be told. People who are forgotten are resentful.

Who Should Tell?

1. Telling is best accepted from one's immediate superior.

2. Where choice is possible in who should tell, always choose a person who is highly acceptable personally, and who has a record for telling things clearly, interestingly, and acceptably to the hearers.

3. While it may conflict with unity of command, we must remember that employees occasionally like to hear your boss or your superior's boss.

What Do You Communicate?

1. We should tell people those facts most calculated to make them feel they belong, that they are an informed and inseparable part of their job, their department, and the company.

2. We should tell those things that will make employees and managers have a feeling both of opportunity and security, that will remove the wonderment, anxiety, and aimless questions that make for confusion, and indifference at work.

3. We should select those things to tell which people will take pride in knowing, which will help satisfy the needs for attention, status, and the feeling of importance.

4. Some say we should tell all that employees will eventually learn by themselves. They say we should do this so that we can tell the facts constructively, truthfully and shaped to whatever purpose we have in mind before others distort the facts through lack of information or for their own ends.

5. We should tell, some say, that there are three categories of facts to be communicated:

a) Those that *must* be told. They are the things that directly or rather immediately affect a man or his job. These include work assignments, flow of work in offices, methods of operation, standards of production, pay, overtime hours, rules and regulations, duties and responsibilities, quality of performance, job security, etc.

b) Those that *should* be told. These are facts a little less directly or less immediately connected with the work operations or the physical conduct of the office or the factory. These facts include knowledge and attitudes necessary to coordinate one's work with that of other people or departments. They deal a little more with the future and with that environment which is a little distant from the job. They include vacation pay, company services, management policy, departmental organization, the place of the job in the whole scheme of things, expected standards of personnel conduct, the finished product, anticipated changes in operations, systems or personnel that influence the man, the job or the department.

c) Those things that *it would be nice to tell*. These might be thought of by some as luxury items. They deal broadly with the company, its organization, its leaders, its economy, its plans for growth and expansion, the company production line, its advertising, sales, research, legal, manufacturing departments and their problems, broad company policy, the economic order, citizenship, etc.

6. Things that are an absolute necessity for telling on one level may become luxury items for people at another level. There are no hard and fast rules for determining what to tell. Good judgment and knowledge of what the people will want to know should guide.

7. In telling reasons for employee separation, good judgment must be used in order not to needlessly hurt the reputation and welfare of an employee who has been separated for cause.

How to Communicate

1. Success in communication depends upon gaining acceptance of what is said. Therefore, the communicator will carefully plan not only what to tell but how to tell it so as to gain most acceptance.

2. One of the best ways to gain acceptance is to give reasons, reasons which have meaning to those being informed.

3. Where persuasion is needed, the oral word can be more effective than the printed word. There is a better opportunity to observe reaction and adapt your presentation to gain the required end.

4. If the details are complex or if the facts are those which the employees do not want to believe, you might as well expect at the outset that you will have to follow up by a review and a retelling.

5. Keep the channels open both ways, by inviting employee response to your telling. Things will go *down* a lot easier if you welcome a few observations and opinions flowing *up*, even unpleasant ones.

6. In planning to communicate always seek for more than one media. A meeting which is reinforced by a letter sent home or a poster which is reinforced with an announcement over the P.A. system is startlingly more effective than an announcement which gets only one treatment.

APPENDIX B

METHODS USED IN STUDY

THE basic objective of this study was to give more substance to the definition of communications in industry by exploring the operation of communications within specific industrial enterprises. The first problem involved the choice of situations to be studied. Two major limitations on wholly free choice immediately were evident: (1) the practical need of choosing situations within easy commuting distance from Princeton; and (2) the necessary agreement of both management and union to cooperate with the research agency.

If any evidence was needed to support the assumption that the cooperation of both parties could be secured only when reasonably friendly union-management relations existed, such evidence quickly appeared in preliminary moves seeking likely situations for study. Thus one of the controlling factors in the choice of cases predetermined that the study should be within the background of peaceful labor relations rather than in a conflict situation. This fact must be understood by the reader in attempting to relate the findings of each case or the general conclusions to problems of communications in other organizations.

Given the specific objectives of studying the purposes of and reactions to the media of communications as well as the media themselves, the methods to be followed were fairly well indicated. Management and union officers whose ideas largely determine the scope and content of downward communication would have to be interviewed. Discussions with them and careful study of the media and channels employed by them in turn would affect the method of approach to the intermediary personnel and the questions to be asked employees.

In the first study, interviews with individuals determining or influencing policy began on the company side with the director and assistant director of personnel, went up to the chairman of the board and down through the president and vice president. On the union side, interviews were principally with local and regional officers but included discussions with two representatives of the international staff of the Textile Workers.

In the second study, company interviews began with refinery line and staff officers, went up to the personnel staff of the New York office of Esso Standard Oil Company and to the personnel staff of the parent corporation, Standard Oil Company (New Jersey). Top refinery executives were interviewed intensively. Since the Independent Petroleum Workers have no national affiliation, all union interviews were at the local level.

As the first case study progressed, it became increasingly clear that advance definitions could not be cut and dried. In spite of attempts to make clear the objectives and limits of the study, the individuals being interviewed placed emphasis on those aspects of the subject of most concern to them.

Consequently the research had continually to be kept in balance between predetermined objectives and pressures developed in the interviews to broaden the scope of or give some special slant to the study. Judgment necessarily played a part in maintaining this balance.

In analyzing the use of the intermediary line organizations as channels of communications, the aim was to get information to compare what the top officials, on the one hand, and employees, on the other, wanted of their supervisors and stewards with what these first-line management and union representatives thought their own roles to be. Guided interviews for supervisors and stewards seemed logical and were used at Johnson & Johnson. However, several indications suggesting a different method emerged. The information sought was sufficiently factual so that little was gained by personal interviews. A questionnaire covering a much larger percentage of foremen (below department head) and stewards might have produced more information with less effort. Open questions, it was believed, would allow for as many volunteered ideas as were gained in the short, guided interviews. The information received could be quantified more readily. Accordingly, information from supervisors and stewards in the Esso study was sought through questionnaires that were closely related to the employee questionnaire.

The employee questionnaire was viewed as the core of both case studies. The aim was to secure, through carefully framed questions, some measurement of the amount of offered information absorbed by employees and their attitude towards the informational efforts of management and union. Planning for the employee poll was facilitated by the advice on technical problems and methodology received from Professor Hadley Cantril of the Department of Psychology of the University. With management and union cooperation, an adequate sampling of employees was assured. Nevertheless the representativeness of any sample can always be questioned, and certain weaknesses in this respect in the two case studies should be pointed out.

The most important limitation, especially for the Johnson & Johnson study, was the high percentage of English illiteracy or near-illiteracy among the older, foreign-born employees. The sample there failed to represent approximately 15 per cent of the workers who could neither read nor write English and among whom a knowledge of company and union policies might be less than average. The recognized near-illiterates were a much lower percentage of the refinery employees, and no sorting out for illiteracy was done in the random sampling. The 12 ballots that had to be discarded from the refinery poll (as compared with one from the Johnson & Johnson poll) may have been due in part to the failure to sort out near-illiterates and in part to other factors, such as individual resentment against being polled.

At Johnson & Johnson, practically all supervisors and stewards were interviewed. The union requested all stewards to report for interview at the union office and the company arranged interviews with all foremen. A few were missed because of chance absenteeism. However, the supervisors interviewed or questionnaired at the Esso refinery were selected by their superiors, and the shop stewards by the union. Thus there may have been some bias towards better than average understanding among these groups.

Another weakness in the poll was the apparent tendency of a few respondents to follow the leadership of some one member of the group in answering particular questions. The members of each group assembled for the poll were made to feel as much at ease as possible. The researcher was, in most instances, introduced in the presence of both union and management representatives to emphasize the impartial nature of the poll. The group was told that the questions were in no way a test of their ability but were developed in an effort to gain their individual understanding of certain facts or policies and their ideas in regard to information given them. They were not forbidden to talk, however, and there was, it appeared, some copying of answers in a few scattered cases.

The greatest difficulty in the use of the questionnaire is the development of the questions. This involves decisions both as to what the questions are to cover and how they are to be phrased. The procedure in both studies was as follows: The field worker developed a tentative list of questions on the basis of the objectives of the study, the information gained through interviews with top management and union personnel as to their objectives in communications, and a study of material issued to employees. This list was reviewed with the research supervisor, and, in the Johnson & Johnson case, with Professor Cantril for general form of questions, and proportion and types of open-end questions. The list was then reviewed with several representatives of union and management, and, in both cases, their recommendations were an important factor in the final choice of questions, within the framework of research objectives, and predetermined length of questionnaire.

The advice of union and management representatives was helpful both in the content and form of the questions. A pre-testing of the employee questionnaire on a small group of employees, and discussion with them following their answering of the questionnaire, resulted in additional rephrasing of a number of questions to make them more readily understood by the worker.

In each case, the code for employee responses was worked out after the poll was taken. Classification for write-in responses was made by the field worker and revised by the supervisor of the research after separate review of the responses. It is recognized that judgment played a large part in this classification, as well as in the interpretation given to the results. The coded replies were transferred to punch cards for tabulation.

Having used unguided and guided interviews and polls of employees in exploring communications in two specific industrial situations, it was necessary to report the findings both quantitatively and impressionistically. Since interviews and questionnaires were worked out within the framework of each situation rather than rigidly according to some predetermined concept, no attempt was made to compare the two studies item by item. Insofar as the findings permitted, however, the two studies were reported in similar form.

Polling results and the information and attitudes learned through the interviews were felt to be meaningful only as related to the total situation. Consequently in preparing the individual reports, considerable attention was given to the company and union organizations and their relationships to each other. Only thus, it was felt, would the reader be able to relate the findings to his own experience and apply them to a solution of his own problems.

RECENT PUBLICATIONS OF THE INDUSTRIAL RELATIONS SECTION

Reports

Transmitting Information through Management and Union Channels. Two case studies. Report Series No. 79. 1949. 141 pp. Paper bound $2.50; Cloth bound $3.00.

Company-wide Understanding of Industrial Relations Policies. A study in communications. Report Series No. 78. 1948. 78 pp. $2.00.

Company Wage Policies. A survey of practice and experience. Report Series No. 77. 1948. 45 pp. $1.50.

Management Procedures in the Determination of Industrial Relations Policies. Report Series No. 76. 1948. 81 pp. $2.00.

Constructive Labor Relations. Experience in four firms. Report Series No. 75. 1948. 116 pp. $2.00.

The Operation of Job Evaluation Plans. Report Series No. 74. 1947. 111 pp. $1.50.

Wages under National and Regional Collective Bargaining. Experience in seven industries. Report Series No. 73. 1946. 103 pp. $1.50.

Group Health Insurance and Sickness Benefit Plans in Collective Bargaining. Report Series No. 72. 1945. 89 pp. and charts. $1.50.

Readjustment of Manpower in Industry during the Transition from War to Peace. Report Series No. 71. 1944. 112 pp. $1.50.

Seniority Problems during Demobilization and Reconversion. Report Series No. 70. 1944. 29 pp. 75 cents.

Maximum Utilization of Employed Manpower. A check list of company practice. Report Series No. 68. 1943. 46 pp. and 4 p. check list. $1.00.

Seniority Policies and Procedures as Developed through Collective Bargaining. Report Series No. 63. 1941. 63 pp. $1.00.

Bibliographies

A Trade Union Library. Bibliographical Series No. 80. (Revised) June, 1949. 54 pp. 75 cents.

Social Security. Bibliographical Series No. 78. (Revised) April, 1947. 57 pp. 75 cents.

The Office Library of an Industrial Relations Executive. Bibliographical Series No. 77. (Revised) March, 1946. 36 pp. 50 cents.

Employment Tests in Industry and Business. Bibliographical Series No. 67. (Revised) April, 1945. 41 pp. 50 cents.

Problems of Reemployment and Retraining of Manpower during the Transition from War to Peace. Bibliographical Series No. 75. (Revised) March, 1945. 44 pp. 50 cents.

Sickness Benefits and Group Purchase of Medical Care for Industrial Employees. Bibliographical Series No. 76. 1944. 28 pp. 30 cents.

Selected References: Issued bi-monthly. 4 pp. 10 cents each, Nos. 1-24; beginning with No. 25, 15 cents each. Annual subscription 75 cents.

Subject Index of the Library of the Industrial Relations Section. (Revised) 1945. 46 pp. 75 cents.

Complete list of available publications, including titles of individual issues of *Selected References*, will be sent on request.